AT HOME WITH CAROLYNE ROEHM

AT HOME WITH CAROLYNE ROEHM

WRITTEN WITH MELISSA DAVIS

PHOTOGRAPHY BY SYLVIE BECQUET, ALAN RICHARDSON, AND ANNE DAY
DESIGN BY DINA DELL'ARCIPRETE HOUSER

BROADWAY BOOKS NEW YORK

Broadway Books titles may be purchased for business or promotional use or for

special sales. For information, please write to: Special Markets Department,

Random House, Inc., 1540 Broadway, New York, NY 10036.

Visit our web site at www.broadwaybooks.com

PHOTO CREDITS **Cover:** Sylvie Becquet. **Back cover:** Eric Bowman. **Endpaper, front,**
title page, dedication: Sylvie Becquet. **Contents:** Alan Richardson and Sylvie Becquet.
Sylvie Becquet: 9, 11, 19-23, 33-39, 40-44, 46, 47, 49, 51-55, 61-68, 71, 72, 74-77, 83, 89-91,
97-102, 104, 105, 107-110, 112, 113, 115-118, 120-122, 124-127, 129-133, 135-140, 142,
144-149, 151-153, 156, 158, 163-165, 170-175, 180-183, 185-188, 190-192, 194-199, 201-203,
205-207, 209-213, 220-222, 225-228, 230-233, 235, 237, 239, 241, 243, 245, 250, 252-257,
259, 261-271, 274-276, 279, 280, 282, 283, 286, 289-291, 293. 294, 296-298, 300. 301, 304,
309, 310, 313, 314, 317. **Alan Richardson:** 12, 13, 24, 26, 27, 28-31, 56, 58, 59, 80, 85, 275,
277, 284, 285, 304, 313. **Anne Day:** 10, 214, 216-219, 317. **Carolyne Roehm:** 244,
Endpaper, back

Recipes by Nancy Quattrini.

Library of Congress Cataloging-in-Publication data
Roehm, Carolyne.
    At Home with Carolyne Roehm/Carolyne Roehm.
        p.cm.
    Includes index.
    ISBN 0-7679-0888-0
      1. Entertaining. 2. Cookery. I.Title
TX731 .R539 2001
642'.4--dc21
                              2001025996

FIRST EDITION
10 9 8 7 6 5 4 3 2 1

To Pookie and Annie
and the rest of the beloved pups.

After thirty years of entertaining, I've learned how to appease the gnawing anxiety that plagues nearly anyone who has ever held a dinner party, a brunch, a formal luncheon, or any celebration that involves a meal. I've learned to deal with holiday performance anxiety, and grappled with those questions that lurk in the mind of nearly every hostess. Why do some tabletops look so "put together" and others like an overloaded jumble of stuff? How do I take various decorative elements—flowers, dishes, linens, et cetera—and combine them with other elements to create a cohesive whole that tells a story? What do I need to do to create a successful and memorable event, whether it's a brown-bag picnic or a grand holiday dinner? How do I decide on a menu that doesn't put too much stress on my guests or me? In the following pages I hope to answer those questions, drawing from examples of how I entertain in my home, Weatherstone, in northwest Connecticut, and my homes in New York City and Paris. This is not a book that addresses only the well-padded pocketbook: I want to emphasize that the same focus on detail applies to a budget-minded informal dinner for a few friends as it does to a grand extravaganza.

INTRODUCTION

Entertaining is one of the last rituals left in our modern, hectic, technological, schedule-stressed life that slows us down. A beautifully decorated table is like a wrapped present, an offering to guests, thanking them for coming to the table.

Entertaining draws us together with family, friends, and strangers to celebrate two primal human needs: socialization and food. Although fashions in dining evolve—we no longer eat out of a communal bowl as we did in ancient times— we still adhere to the belief that sharing food is good and right. Even prehistoric man killed his prey, then dragged it back to the group, giving thanks to the gods for the sacrifice. Throughout history, we have gone through elaborate protocols to express the breaking of our bread. Descriptions of eighteenth-century French banquets or Roman bacchanalia read like overproduced spec-

tacles rife with prescribed behaviors and accoutrements. The elaborate table settings—from fish forks to cruet stands—and manners of middle-class Victorians seem terribly strained to the modern eye.

How we have evolved   But have we really changed so much in our ways of gathering at the table? Fast-food gobbling aside, we are still more careful in our speech, more fastidious in our cleanliness, and more exacting with our implements than is necessary simply to eat to sustain life. So why do we bother to place various glasses for wine, press and starch the white linens, and arrange flowers for the centerpiece? Because how we go about sharing one of life's necessities is what separates us from animals. We seem driven to distinguish ourselves from those below us on the food chain. Even so-called primitive cultures "present" food, if only on a banana leaf. Saying grace before a meal is no different from the Neanderthal who would not eat until he bowed to the gods for providing the mastodon. Since we must kill to eat, perhaps we rid ourselves of guilt by forming rituals that say we are sorry for the necessary violence. We may have removed ourselves from the hunt, but the ancient rituals of thanks have grown into the manners and elements of the modern table.

My philosophy on entertaining   It is difficult to dissect the ineffable dazzle of a well-dressed table, but if you examine the photos in this book, you will see that each setting has a theme supported by many details. The inspiration for the theme—the colors and textures, the level of formality, the food—might be the season, but it may also come from a favorite color combination, a painting, a holiday, a piece of fabric, a flower, or a beloved heirloom. Once I have settled on the theme, I do not stray. You can lay your table with the best of the best, but if you ignore your theme's boundaries, none of that expensive tableware will tell a cohesive story. It will just be a jarring jumble of fine tablecloth, crystal, and china. Repetition of a single element on the tabletop is more effective than loading down the stage with an onslaught of colors and textures. The less-is-more mantra stands true. Also, less is not only more, less is much easier if you are too busy for more.

This rule applies to the food as well as to the tabletop. My simple menus are drawn from what is freshest and in season, not from what is in vogue or rare or fussy. The recipes in this book were gathered from friends and family, adapted from various cooking class instructions, and improved upon by collaboration with Nancy Quattrini and Margarida de Carvalho, the Weatherstone cooks.

I may adhere to an entertaining theme, but I don't stick to the concept of dining in the "dining room." If my tabletop thesis doesn't mesh with the formal dining room, I simply move the table to the center hall, the library, the living room, or whatever space fits my theme. To avoid having to collect a series of different-size tablecloths, my mobile dining room table is sixty inches in diameter—a common dimension for tablecloth manufacturers—which easily seats ten. More than ten at a table creates conversation puddles.

Once I have decided on the theme of the table, I choose the dinner plates. The color pattern of the plates often determines the flowers chosen for the centerpiece, and for the other decorative elements on the table.

Finally, because the passing of seasons plays such an important part in my life—they dictate what food I eat and what flowers I choose— I have divided the book into summer, fall, winter, and springtime entertaining. Within each season are examples of specific tabletops and menus that illustrate the best way to take advantage of that season's food and themes.

How the book works

I view entertaining as a creative outlet, a theater set waiting to be designed before the play opens. When the audience arrives, I want them to feel, as they move from cocktails to dinner to after-dinner coffee, as if the production were seamless, effortless, and graceful.

Carolyne Roehm

SPRING

Spring means to leap into being, to stretch suddenly, to explode. that season, as well as does to my soul. Afte starved for something monochromatic scale of color—no matter h for enthusiastic celeb

r bound, to come
r bend, to arise
The definition fits
what the season
endless gray days,
off that dingy
the arrival of a thing
w humble—is cause
ration.

1

A Formal Celebration of Spring
THE CAMELLIA DINNER

In very early spring, the half-dozen hothouse camellia plants unveil their perfect blooms. It is such an anticipated event, and the blossoms are so scarce, that they became the impetus for this table's theme. I couldn't make a huge splash with so few buds, so I spread out the effect by putting each in its own silver vase or beaker, creating the appearance of the flowers dancing around the centerpiece. To create my setting, I moved a library table into the center hall, knowing the weathered door would make a perfect backdrop, and I flanked the door with Zen-like bows of forced pink quince.

AT dusk the atmosphere dims. The mood of the table changes and becomes more seductive. William Yeoward's crystal glasses, a collection of silver vases, Irish linen napkins with a damask border, and eighteenth-century Wedgwood creamware, create an environment of simple, not fussy, elegance. The color theme—blue, white, silver, and pink—may look cohesive, but the components are a conscious textural mix-and-match of old and new, tall and short, icy and smooth, deeply etched and lightly feathered.

Icy silvers and crystal whites embolden the innocence of pink camellias.

the Menu

Asparagus in Puff Pastry with Lemon Sauce*

Veal Scallops with Morels and Cream*

Spaetzle

Salad of Early Spring Lettuce

Strawberry Pavlova*

1996 Louis Latour Corton-Charlemagne
Grand Cru, Burgundy

Asparagus in puff pastry fools the eye as well as the palate. The recipe is simplicity itself to prepare with the help of frozen pastry, and delicious, thanks to the lemony butter sauce.

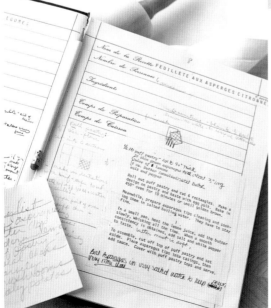

WHEN deciding the menu for the camellia dinner, seasonality was paramount: morels, asparagus, strawberries, and baby lettuce were at their peak. The morel season is so painfully short that I was anxious to incorporate them into the dinner. I translated my midwestern childhood memories of creamed morels on toast into a sauce for the veal.

VEAL SCALLOPS WITH MORELS AND CREAM

A Midday Salute to

EASTER IN THE COUNTRY

Easter in northwest Connecticut does not conjure clichéed images of spring. The daffodils struggle to push up through the frozen ground, robin sightings are scarce, and the asparagus sleeps. If fortune—and global warming—is on my side, I may see twinges of spring three weeks after the March solstice, but nothing substantial enough to clip or harvest. Therefore, the first holiday of spring must borrow from the city flower mart. Daffodils, anemones, and pansies, which take precedence on the table, come north in abundance at this time. The henhouse cooperates, and the smooth white eggs lead me to the theme of the table: plain white ceramic to showcase the spring flowers.

I splurge on the rabbit-embossed menu cards (left), but save on the table decorations: a dozen white eggs and a six-pack of pansies. Pansies show up early at the local garden center. I pop them out of their plastic cartons and repot them in milk glass beakers (below left). A mix of double and single daffodils and anemones fill the white milk pitcher (opposite).

Until April's showers bring May flowers, Easter bouquets of jolly daffs and anemones must come from the city flower district.

the Menu

Green Cauliflower Soup with Pita Triangles*

Roasted Leg of Lamb Marinated with Fresh Herbs*

Potatoes Anna*

Caramelized Bananas with Toasted Coconut and Lime*

Pecan Cookies

1997 Elderton Shiraz, Barossa Valley,
   South Australia

ALWAYS mindful of the season's best offerings, Nancy Quattrini, the cook at Weatherstone, creates a delicate cauliflower soup and elevates the simple spud to artwork. The spiraled slices of sautéed potatoes (below right), achieved with a $15 mandoline, feed the eye with little effort at the stove.

PLAIN WHITE CHINA AND CLEAR GLASS PLATES ARE THE EQUIVALENT OF THE LITTLE BLACK DRESS. IF YOU CAN AFFORD NO OTHER, THESE TWO BASICS SHOULD BE THE FOUNDATION OF YOUR TABLE.

The flavor of caramelized sugar harmonizes with vanilla ice cream.
Crunch of coconut offers texture, while the zest brings zing.

Celadon and White Create

A PARISIAN DINNER

I am fortunate to have the luxury of being able to visit Paris frequently, where, until recently, I have kept a small apartment. I am drawn to Paris for two reasons: the unsurpassed fresh-flower market at Rungis and the twice-weekly food market next to the Champs Mars. The French astound me with their sensitivity to cut flowers and food. When I buy cheese, for instance, the vendor quizzes me: When will I eat the cheese? What will I serve with it? Then he tells me the best wine to drink to enhance the cheese's flavor. This attention to what is ripe, and right, and ready makes shopping for food and flowers something of an educational adventure. My other favorite activity is watching the unfolding street scene from one of my favorite rooms, painted in celadon green and white, which faces the road at tree level. A set of French doors opens to a small balcony, and from there I observe the comings and goings on the Avenue de Ségur.

*Viburnum, hydrangea, anemone, and a painted tulip display
tints of white, pink, apricot, and new green.*

WHEN I spied these decorative white porcelain (reproduction)

soup bowls (opposite) at the Louvre gift shop, I knew they would make a long-lasting marriage with the white porcelain plates I had bought some years earlier. The delicate floral detailing agrees with the matelassé tablecloth, and easily segues to the white porcelain câchepots and candlesticks. Sprays of forced white prunus, which I had picked up at Rungis, the wholesale flower market outside Paris, seem to explode from the brass nineteenth-century urn.

the Menu

LOBSTER BISQUE

GRILLED BABY LAMB CHOPS

ASPARAGUS IN LEMON BUTTER

BERRIES AND RED CURRANTS

   WITH GRAND MARNIER SAUCE*

1995 HUDELOT-NOELLAT BOURGOGNE ROUGE,

   BURGUNDY

Red currants, blueberries, and spring's best strawberries topped with Grand Marnier sauce.

Beneath the Orchard Boughs

A PICNIC WITH FRIENDS

So much backbreaking digging—more than ten years and ten thousand bulbs—has gone into seeding the orchard with daffodils, that I make sure to appreciate every minute of their short blooming season. An excellent way to celebrate the arrival of the daffs is to organize a picnic beside their nodding heads. Children seem to delight in the wide variety of cups and petals even more than the adults do. My friend Susana helped me gather a centerpiece from the field, which we tucked into a bucket hidden by a basket. With a snip of pinking shears, a length of raffia, and a few stray daffs, our brown-bag lunch became a delightful, well-dressed treat. None of the elements was fussy, but everyday paper, tin, and glass were primped up for the presentation.

A humble brown bag turns into a fancy satchel with the addition of pinked edges, raffia ties, and a solo narcissus.

the Menu

Biscuit Sandwiches of Mustard-Glazed Ham
  and Smoked Cheddar*

Dilled Potato Salad with Vinaigrette

Crudités Baskets

Aunt June's Lemon Bars*

Mason Jar Iced Tea

1998 Les Hautes Muscadet Côtes de Grandlieu sur Lie

RATTAN

basket trays (opposite) hold jars of iced tea and crudités, a biscuit sandwich, and a Chinese takeout carton of potato salad. Biscuits wrapped in deli paper, which was also used to line the takeout cartons (below) and wrap the lemon squares (below right) were secured with raffia. A galvanized tin tub from the local feed store holds an afternoon's worth of iced tea (top right) served in canning jars.

AN UNCOMPLICATED TRIP TO THE SUPERMARKET YIELDS THE INGREDIENTS FOR THE PICNIC LUNCH, INCLUDING MASON JARS, BAGGED ICE, AND DELI PAPER.

Daffodil Spotlight on

AN EARLY LUNCH

In late April, when the daffodils under the orchard finally bloom, my efforts from a decade of fall bulb planting finally pay off. For three weeks, I fill every vase, basket, pitcher, and câchepot in my possession with armfuls of jonquils and daffs. The mass blooms are a spectacular indulgence. To bounce their brilliance, I display them on a field of blue and white matelassé: Blue represents the sky, white the clouds, and yellow the sun. I have captured a fine spring day. I selected reproduction Regency crystal to formalize the setting, and marked each place with a minibouquet of daffodils set in an inexpensive reproduction blue-and-white vase.

*Celebrate the colors of the spring sky
with an oversized collection of daffodils and
mimosa surrounded by blue and white.*

6

Lilies of the Fete

MOTHER'S DAY

Lily of the valley surely rates with dandelions as one of the first flowers we pick as children to present to our mother. I speak from experience. They were the first blooms I stole from the neighbor's garden to offer my own mother. With its heady scent and nodding white bells—and generous willingness to naturalize easily—*Convallaria majalis,* or *muguet* in France, where I set this table, offers much more than its daintiness advertises. I have been so taken with this flower that I designed a series of linens embroidered with its likeness to dress the spring table. On Mother's Day, my mother joined me in Paris, and I toasted her with blooming lily of the valley plants nestled in a wire basket footed in moss. Service plates were topped with St. Cloud–inspired porcelain beakers holding more of the same.

Splendor in the Grass

A LATE BREAKFAST

Once the warm weather arrives, it takes a mean force of nature to drive me indoors. For the next six months, few meals will be eaten under a roof, unless a wisteria-covered pergola counts. Al fresco dining does require a bit more muscle—dragging tables and food from pond, to pool, to patio—but after such a long winter, I feel the extra effort is worth it. Much of my outdoor tableware must be unbreakable, so I am always on the hunt for attractive rattan, wood, and anything-not-plastic that travels well. When I discovered the tin enamelware camp plates, I knew I was onto a good thing, especially since the dinnerware mates so well with ubiquitous bistro flatware and does little damage to the pocketbook. To bring the grass-and-wildflower pasture closer to the table, I added a more fragile majolica pitcher of wild daisies.

*To dine in a field of tall pasture grasses is
like having a picnic amid a sea of wild fairies.*

FOR outdoor dining, inexpensive enameled splatterware (also known as graniteware, speckled-relishware, or pickleware) is a much more attractive picnic alternative to plastic or paper. Graniteware has been used in American homes since the early nineteenth century. Earlier graniteware was green or turquoise blue with gray spatters, the same background later followed with white spatters. It is now widely available in a variety of colors. If actual use is more important than display, I find the modern reproductions superior.

A platter of plump, ripe strawberries fulfills a decorative as well as a practical purpose.

the Menu

Margarida's Frittata*

Maple-Cured Bacon

Biscuits and Strawberry Jam

Fresh Garden Strawberries

Coffee and Tea

Tulips and Mangoes Dress Up

DINNER IN THE COUNTRY

Thematic cues for spring dining don't have to be all bunny-fluffy sweetness and light pastels. More serious tones can carry the decor. When the tulips, following the daffodils, bloom, I let their bold purples, oranges, reds, and apricots tell me what to do. My particular favorites, the painted Rembrandts and flashy parrots, look as if they jumped off the canvas of a Dutch master. So as not to detract from the tulips' flamboyance, I decided on muted earthy yellow Provençal pottery plates, which led my eye to the blushing ocher mangoes that I casually scattered at the base of the tulip arrangements. The bamboo-handled flatware also borrow from the straw-colored spectrum. Dandelion greens were in season, and I knew they would look good on the plate with green napkins and green-rimmed Mexican glasses.

Bone, bamboo, rattan, and ocher-glazed pottery plates meld with the rustic flavor of the bare wooden farm table.

THE idea to use any seasonal fruit or vegetables, mangoes in this case, as a table decoration is most effective when the same produce is also used as an ingredient. For instance, in late summer, when the basil peaks, I place bouquets of the herb on the table near a plate of pesto-topped pasta. Or, what could be more sensual than a collection of pink, purple, green, white, or magenta eggplants to highlight a moussaka feast?

the Menu

Seared Sesame Tuna with Pear-Mango Salsa*

Dandelion Greens with Bacon and Garlic*

Key Lime Pie

Assortment of Imported Beers

1997 Crichton Hall Chardonnay, Napa Valley

Fleeting Pink Peonies Amid
A LIGHT LUNCH

Peony season is short and fragile. The blowsy blooms display their powers in early June, but so do black clouds overhead, which release damaging rains and push the faces of the blossoms into the mud. Armed with pruning shears, I do my best to behead the flowers before the spring showers do their worst. I gather the opulent white, pink, red, and garnet flowers and fill the house; the scent permeates every room. This is a sensation that must be shared. A ladies' lunch suits; the feminine perfume and ballerina pink poofs might make the men nervous. At the table, mid-pink 'Sarah Bernhardt' peonies held in celadon tinware cups charm us all.

A mass of blooms or a single stem . . . as a cut flower, herbaceous peonies have no equal.

the Menu

MARGARIDA'S PORTUGUESE CLAMS*

WATERCRESS, RED ONION, AND CUCUMBER SALAD

CRUSTY COUNTRY BREAD

PASSION FRUIT SORBET

1998 ANDRE RAFFAITIN SANCERRE, LOIRE VALLEY

10

Under the Willow Tree

A SECRET SPRING DINNER

Creative al fresco dining requires that you think outside the boxed patio. Drop prescribed rules of defined outdoor space. Find a corner of the garden that gives you pleasure. Even a postage stamp of a backyard can hide a cozy niche or a handsome view. Pose your table as if you were creating a tableau vivant. Children know that weeping branches make excellent secret houses. Remember dragging cardboard boxes and milk crates to a burrow in a hidden thicket when you were young? Recall those memories when creating an outdoor dining room. On this clear day, a canopy of willow leaves afforded filtered light while reminding me of those childhood hideaways.

*Lacy cremeware enhances the dappled light
provided by the slender new-green willow leaves.*

the *Menu*

Cumin-Scented Asparagus Soup*

Grilled Spicy Moroccan Chicken with Quinoa*

Asparagus with Lemon Confit*

Strawberry Pavlova*

1998 Saddleback Cellars Viognier

An abundant asparagus crop yields a light soup garnished with tips and lemon zest (above left), and a citrus-tinged side dish (above right). Another spring garden crop: Strawberries lie on a bed of meringue (opposite) garnished with mint tips.

Borrowing from Spring for

A SPECIAL FORMAL MEAL

For many of my tables, I cheat. I recycle curtains and bedspreads for tablecloths, slip in pieces of museum-shop reproduction china, use plain houseware-outlet glasses, or pinch roadside botanicals for my centerpiece. The provenance of humble hotel napkins and three-dollar wineglasses can be effectively masked with a sharp pressing or a careful buffing. But sometimes a benchmark birthday or anniversary demands that I pull out all the stops: eighteenth-century Paul Storr flatware and service plates, Baccarat crystal, hand-embroidered linens, and delicate Italian ceramic table accessories. Once the man-made elements are in place, I might add a perfect sprig of lilac or a spray of wisteria at each place as the only spot of color. Nature's riches, I'm happily reminded, often upstage my extravagant efforts.

Pink Peony Parade at
AN AL FRESCO LUNCH

As much as I love playing with color, texture, and detail, I also love to strip
ornamentation from the table to create a modern silhouette. A field of
stark white plates and accessories shouts streamlined minimalism, but
individual pieces adapt to fussier schemes. This explains why white plates
are a tabletop basic. An all-glass table setting achieves the same cool effect.
Sober clear dishes grounded on a stark white tablecloth look chic and clean.
Glass is an honest medium; it conceals nothing, but reflects everything.
I must be cautious with its use. Runny sauces, oily foods, and complicated
presentations don't fit its properties. Glass-cylinder vases reveal leggy
stems; I am as mindful of their arrangement as I am of the peony bud.

THE three-week peony season continues, and again I showcase their charms. My last peony feature played with a favorite combination of celadon and same-color pink. This lunch shows off the peonies in all their glorious color combinations, and I did not want to distract from that diversity. Using a glass theme, I was able to make the various colors of the flowers bounce from the reflective platform and fill the table with shards of color.

Enliven a cool glass of lemonade with a snip of mint and a citrus slice.

ZUCCHINI AND WATERCRESS SOUP*

WHITE BEAN AND SHRIMP SALAD*

COCONUT CAKE*

MINTED LEMONADE

1999 ADEGAS MORGADIO ALBARINO,

RIAS BAIXAS, GALICIA

I wanted the menu to be as simple and springlike as the table, but I also wanted the colors of the food to fit the glassy theme, so I adjusted the meal accordingly. Pale green soup, white beans and shrimp on a bed of crinkled spinach, and a white cake iced in downy coconut all borrowed from the same color pool and harmonized perfectly.

A CHILLED WATERCRESS SOUP (ABOVE LEFT) AND SALAD ENTRÉE (OPPOSITE) ARE AIRY ENOUGH TO ALLOW AN INDULGENT DESSERT OF COCONUT CAKE (ABOVE RIGHT).

ASPARAGUS IN PUFF PASTRY WITH LEMON SAUCE

THE CAMELLIA DINNER *page 22*

6 servings

½ pound frozen puff pastry,
    thawed overnight in refrigerator
1 egg yolk beaten with 1 teaspoon water

36 thin asparagus stalks
Juice of 1 lemon
2 sticks unsalted butter, softened
Salt and white pepper to taste

1. Preheat oven to 425° F. Unwrap puff pastry. On a lightly floured surface, roll out pastry to a 12-inch square, a scant ¼ inch thick. Cut pastry into 6 rectangles and score in a lattice pattern with a sharp knife. With a metal spatula, transfer rectangles to a cookie sheet and brush with egg yolk, avoiding the edges of the pastry. Bake for 10 minutes or until golden. Cool.

2. Meanwhile, snap off woody ends of asparagus and trim tips to about 3 inches in length. Steam or boil in heavily salted water until al dente, 2 to 3 minutes. Drain.

3. In a small pan, heat the lemon juice over low flame. Add butter slowly, whisking all the time until the sauce becomes smooth and creamy. Do not let boil. Remove from heat and season with salt and pepper.

4. Cut puff pastry rectangles in half horizontally. Place six stalks of cooked asparagus on the bottom half of each pastry rectangle. Pour lemon-butter sauce over each serving and top with the other half of pastry.

VEAL SCALLOPS WITH MORELS AND CREAM

THE CAMELLIA DINNER *page 22*

6 servings

1 cup all-purpose flour
2 teaspoons salt
2 teaspoons pepper
Unsalted butter
Olive oil
6 tablespoons minced shallots

1½ to 2 pounds fresh or 4 ounces dried morels*
3 pounds veal scaloppini (12 slices
    pounded ¼ inch thick)
3 cups veal or mushroom broth
1 cup heavy cream
¼ cup chopped chervil

1. Combine flour, salt, and pepper on a large plate.

2. In a large skillet, melt 3 tablespoons butter and 3 tablespoons olive oil over moderate heat. Dredge scaloppini slices in flour; shake off excess. Lightly brown a few veal slices at a time on both sides, about 1 minute each. Keep slices warm on a platter covered with foil as you go along. Add more butter and olive oil as needed to sauté slices.

3. In the same skillet, sauté shallots for 3 or 4 minutes until softened. Add morels. Season with salt and pepper to taste. Sauté 3 more minutes.

4. Add veal or, if you used the dried morels, the reserved mushroom broth and the cream and reduce over high heat until you have approximately 2 cups of liquid. Pour over veal slices, garnish with chervil, and serve.

*If using dried morels, rinse thoroughly with cold water and reconstitute in 4 cups of warm water for 2 hours. Let the sand settle and reserve the top 3 cups of broth.

STRAWBERRY PAVLOVA

THE CAMELLIA DINNER *page 22*

6 to 8 servings
7 egg whites
1½ teaspoons white vinegar
1½ cups superfine sugar
½ cup confectioners' sugar

1 quart strawberries, topped and sliced
¼ cup plus 2 tablespoons granulated sugar
1 pint heavy cream
1 teaspoon vanilla

1. Preheat the oven to 275° F. With an electric mixer, beat egg whites until firm. Continue beating as you slowly add vinegar and superfine sugar. Beat until egg whites are stiff and shiny. Fold in confectioners' sugar.
2. Line a cookie sheet with parchment paper. Fill a pastry bag with meringue. Pipe the meringue (as shown in photograph, page 69) along the lined cookie sheet until you have a decorative base.
3. Bake meringue shell for 2 hours, or until slightly golden. Cool. Peel off parchment paper and set meringue on a large platter.
4. In a medium saucepan on low heat, cook half the sliced strawberries, with ¼ cup granulated sugar for 15 minutes. Cool completely.
5. Begin whipping heavy cream. When it starts to thicken, add vanilla and continue whipping until stiff peaks form. Add the 2 tablespoons sugar just before you finish.
6. Carefully fold strawberry sauce into whipped cream. Pour mixture into meringue shell. Top with the remaining strawberries and serve.

GREEN CAULIFLOWER SOUP WITH PITA TRIANGLES

EASTER IN THE COUNTRY *page 29*

4 to 6 servings
3 tablespoons olive oil, plus some for pita triangles
1 cup chopped shallots
2 garlic cloves, coarsely chopped
1 large potato, peeled and cubed
1 head green cauliflower, separated into florets
1 quart chicken broth
1 cup heavy cream

2 tablespoons lime juice
1 teaspoon salt
1 teaspoon white pepper
⅛ teaspoon cayenne
3 pita bread rounds
¼ cup chopped cilantro
2 tablespoons lime zest

1. In a large saucepan, heat 3 tablespoons olive oil over medium-high heat. Add shallots and garlic and sauté until translucent.
2. Add potato and cauliflower. Sauté for 3 more minutes.
3. Add chicken broth and bring to a boil. Reduce heat and simmer until potatoes are tender.
4. Add heavy cream, lime juice, salt, pepper, and cayenne. Set aside to cool.
5. Puree soup in a food processor or with an immersion blender until smooth.
6. Preheat the oven broiler. Brush pita with olive oil. Sprinkle pita with cilantro and place under the broiler for 1 minute. Cut pita into triangles. Gently reheat soup, garnish with lime zest, and serve with pita triangles.

THE REFRESHING LIME-GREEN CAULIFLOWER (LEFT) KEEPS ITS COLOR DURING COOKING. YOU HAVE THE
OPTION OF ROASTING THE LEG OF LAMB (RIGHT) WITH REAMED ORANGE HALVES. IF YOU CAN FIND BLOOD
ORANGES, THEY WILL GIVE A SHARPER TASTE TO THE MARINADE.

ROASTED LEG OF LAMB MARINATED WITH FRESH HERBS

EASTER IN THE COUNTRY *page 29*

8 servings

10 garlic cloves, peeled

2 cups red table wine

Juice of 6 oranges, or 2 cups orange juice

5 sprigs of fresh rosemary

8 sprigs of fresh thyme

8 to 10 whole black peppercorns

8- to 10-pound leg of lamb

Salt and freshly ground pepper to taste

½ cup orange juice

1 cup chicken broth

2 tablespoons tomato paste

¼ cup peach or red currant jam or orange marmalade

1. Mix the garlic, wine, orange juice, rosemary, thyme, and peppercorns in a bowl. Place leg of lamb in a
roasting pan and pour marinade over lamb. Let marinate for 1 hour.

2. Preheat oven to 450° F. Pour off marinade from roasting pan and reserve. Salt and pepper the lamb and place
garlic, rosemary, and thyme from marinade atop meat.

3. Roast for 40 to 45 minutes. Reduce heat to 375° F and bake for another 45 minutes. (Total cooking time is
about 10 minutes per pound.)

4. Strain marinade through a fine wire mesh, pressing pulp with a wooden spoon. Pour marinade into a small
saucepan and add ½ cup orange juice and the chicken broth. Reduce over medium heat until you have 1 cup of
sauce. Add tomato paste and jam or marmalade to reduced marinade and simmer until the jam is dissolved.
Serve sparingly with the lamb.

POTATOES ANNA

EASTER IN THE COUNTRY *page 29*

6 servings

2 tablespoons butter

1 tablespoon olive oil

3 russet potatoes, peeled and washed

Salt and freshly ground pepper to taste

Sprigs of fresh herbs such as thyme, rosemary, or
    tarragon (optional)

Parmigiano-Reggiano cheese (optional)

1. Using a mandoline, or the thinnest slicing blade on a food processor, slice the potatoes ⅛ inch thick. Pat slices dry with paper towels.

2. Heat the butter and olive oil in a 12-inch, nonstick sauté pan over low heat. Remove the pan from the stove and overlap the potato slices (like a fanned deck of cards) in a spiral pattern at the bottom of the sauté pan, making the spiral about ½ inch smaller than the circumference of the pan. Season the potatoes with salt and pepper. Return the pan to the stove and cook potatoes over the lowest heat possible for about 30 minutes or until brown.

3. To brown the potatoes on the other side, remove the pan from the stove and place a flat pot lid smaller than the pan on top of the potatoes. Invert the pan while holding on to the lid so the disk of potatoes rests on the lid. Slide the potatoes from the lid back into the pan. If the spiral is disturbed, rearrange the potatoes before sliding them back into the pan. Return the pan to low heat and continue cooking until the edges of the disk are crispy but the center is still a bit soft. (While cooking, you may need to flatten the disk with the smaller lid weighted with a brick, or press the potatoes with a spatula.) Correct seasonings and serve immediately. Slices can be cut from the disk with a pizza cutter.

Options: You may decorate the potatoes with small sprigs of herbs in the final stages of cooking. With a spatula, gently lift the potatoes and scoot herbs underneath. Cook for another minute and serve. The potatoes can be dusted with grated Parmigiano-Reggiano cheese.

CARAMELIZED BANANAS WITH TOASTED COCONUT AND LIME

EASTER IN THE COUNTRY *page 29*

6 to 8 servings

½ cup sugar

2 tablespoons unsalted butter

½ cup dark rum

6 tablespoons heavy cream

Juice of ½ lime

4 bananas, sliced diagonally, 1-inch thick

Vanilla ice cream

½ cup unsweetened shredded coconut, lightly toasted

2 tablespoons julienned lime zest

1. Heat a heavy sauté pan over a medium flame. Add sugar and stir with a wooden spoon until the sugar melts and turns medium amber, about 4 minutes. Add butter to stop caramelizing. Be careful, as the mixture is very hot.

2. Add rum and continue stirring until alcohol cooks off. Add cream and stir until smooth. Add lime juice.

3. Add bananas and continue to cook for 2 minutes. Serve atop ice cream and garnish with coconut and lime zest.

BERRIES AND RED CURRANTS WITH GRAND MARNIER SAUCE

A PARISIAN DINNER *page 36*

6 servings

6 egg yolks

½ cup sugar

¼ cup Grand Marnier

1 pint heavy cream, whipped

1 pint blackberries, cleaned

1 pint blueberries, cleaned

1 pint raspberries, cleaned

1 cup strawberries, cleaned and sliced

½ pint red currants, cleaned

1. In a double boiler over medium-high heat, beat egg yolks with sugar until thick and creamy. Whisk in Grand Marnier.

2. Remove from heat. Let cool and fold in whipped cream. Arrange berries in individual bowls and top with Grand Marnier sauce.

BISCUIT SANDWICHES OF MUSTARD-GLAZED HAM AND SMOKED CHEDDAR

A PICNIC WITH FRIENDS *page 41*

6 to 8 servings

1 small boneless ham, about 3 pounds

½ cup honey mustard

1½ cups freshly squeezed orange juice

6 to 8 large buttermilk biscuits

1 pound smoked Cheddar, sliced

1. Preheat oven to 350° F. Place ham in a small roasting pan and brush with honey mustard. Add 1 cup of orange juice to the bottom of the pan and bake ham for 1 hour. Add remaining ½ cup of orange juice during baking (liquid should not evaporate or brown).

2. Remove ham from oven and let rest for 10 minutes. Separate fat from mustard-orange sauce and discard.

3. Cut biscuits in half horizontally and drag cut sides through sauce.

4. Top biscuits with ham and cheddar. Return to oven for approximately 5 minutes or until cheese is melted.

Biscuits are one of the best things to have on hand for quick meals. Use them to make picnic sandwiches filled with ham or with chutney and scraps of sharp cheddar cheese.

AUNT JUNE'S LEMON BARS

A PICNIC WITH FRIENDS *page 41*

Makes 12

1 cup plus 2 tablespoons all-purpose flour

¼ cup confectioners' sugar, plus some for sprinkling

1 stick butter, softened

2 large eggs

1 cup granulated sugar

½ cup fresh lemon juice

½ teaspoon baking powder

1. Preheat oven to 350° F. Whisk together 1 cup flour and the confectioners' sugar.

2. Cut in the softened butter and mix with a fork until the mixture resembles coarse meal. Pat mixture into an 8-inch-square pan. Bake for 20 minutes, but do not turn off oven.

3. Beat eggs with an electric mixer until light and fluffy. Slowly add granulated sugar, 2 tablespoons of flour, lemon juice, and baking powder. Mix well, until completely smooth, and spoon on top of the baked crust. Bake for 25 minutes, then set aside to cool. Sprinkle cooled bars with some confectioners' sugar.

MARGARIDA'S FRITTATA

A LATE BREAKFAST *page 55*

6 to 8 servings

4 russet potatoes

2 tablespoons olive oil

2 garlic cloves, chopped

½ cup each: red peppers, orange peppers, baby
   portobello mushrooms, and onions, coarsely chopped

½ cup peas

½ cup minced parsley

8 large eggs

Salt and freshly ground black pepper to taste

1. Preheat oven to 350° F. Peel and cube potatoes. Parboil in salted water for about 8 minutes. The potatoes should be firm.

2. Heat oil in a large iron skillet over medium heat. Add garlic and sauté until golden. Remove garlic. Add all the vegetables except the potatoes and peas. Sauté for about 8 minutes. Add potatoes and continue to cook for another 3 minutes. Add peas and parsley and continue to sauté for 2 minutes.

3. Beat eggs with salt and pepper. Add beaten eggs to vegetable mixture. Remove skillet from stove.

4. Put egg-vegetable mixture in the oven and bake for about 20 minutes, or until eggs are set. Serve immediately.

SEARED SESAME TUNA WITH PEAR-MANGO SALSA

DINNER IN THE COUNTRY *page 59*

6 servings

2 tablespoons mirin (Japanese rice wine)

3 tablespoons sesame oil

1 tablespoon finely grated ginger

2 tablespoons plus ¼ cup olive oil

6 tuna steaks, about ½ pound each and 1½ inches thick

¼ cup black sesame seeds

¼ cup white sesame seeds

Lime for garnish

1. Whisk together mirin, sesame oil, ginger, and 2 tablespoons olive oil in a small bowl.

2. Place tuna on a platter and spoon marinade over. Marinate in the refrigerator for an hour or two. After steaks have marinated, press mixed sesame seeds into the surface.

3. Put the remaining ¼ cup olive oil in a large cast-iron frying pan (or a nonstick pan) and heat on high until just smoking. Add steaks to the pan (don't let the sides touch) and sear on each side for 4 minutes for medium rare.

4. Garnish with a slice of lime and serve with Pear-Mango Salsa (recipe follows).

Pear-Mango Salsa

1 mango, peeled, seeded, and chopped

2 pears, peeled, cored, and chopped

3 ripe tomatoes, cored, seeded, and chopped

½ medium red onion, diced

Juice and zest of ½ lime

¼ cup minced flat leaf parsley

¼ cup minced cilantro

1 small jalapeño pepper, seeded and diced

Combine all ingredients and let rest for 30 minutes. Serve with seared tuna.

DANDELION GREENS WITH BACON AND GARLIC

DINNER IN THE COUNTRY *page 59*

6 servings

4 strips bacon, finely chopped

2 garlic cloves, coarsely chopped

1 pound dandelion greens, washed and
  coarsely chopped

¼ teaspoon cayenne pepper

1. In a large frying pan over medium-high heat, sauté bacon until almost crisp. Add garlic and sauté for 1 minute. Drain fat from pan, leaving 2 tablespoons.

2. Add greens to bacon-garlic mix and sauté for 3 minutes. Season with cayenne and serve.

THE MILD SEARED TUNA GETS A LIFT FROM MANGO-PEAR SALSA SPIKED WITH JALAPEÑO PEPPERS (LEFT). DANDELIONS (RIGHT), THE BANE OF THE SUBURBAN LAWN, ARE REDEEMED WHEN SAUTÉED WITH BACON AND GARLIC.

MARGARIDA'S PORTUGUESE CLAMS

A LIGHT LUNCH *page 63*

6 servings

¼ cup olive oil

1 medium onion, coarsely chopped

1 garlic clove, coarsely chopped

1 cup diced chorizo

1 bay leaf

1 large sprig of parsley, plus ¼ cup minced

1 tablespoon paprika

1 cup white wine

½ teaspoon red pepper flakes

3 dozen clams

Salt and freshly ground pepper to taste

1. In a large saucepan, heat oil over medium heat. Add onion and garlic and sauté until translucent.

2. Add chorizo and sauté for 2 minutes. Add bay leaf, parsley sprig, paprika, wine, and pepper flakes, and simmer for 5 minutes.

3. Add clams and steam (covered) for 10 minutes, or until clams open. Season with salt and pepper. Sprinkle clams with minced parsley and serve alone or over linguini.

CUMIN-SCENTED ASPARAGUS SOUP

A SECRET SPRING DINNER *page 68*

6 to 8 servings

3 pounds asparagus, peeled and cut into ½-inch pieces

6 cups chicken broth

1 large onion, diced

2 garlic cloves

One 6-ounce can peeled green chili peppers

2 teaspoons ground cumin

Juice of ½ lime

Salt and freshly ground pepper to taste

¼ cup chopped cilantro

1. In a large soup pot, combine the asparagus, chicken broth, onion, and garlic. Bring to a boil. Skim foam from the top and reduce heat. Simmer for 15 minutes.

2. Add chili peppers and cumin and simmer for 5 more minutes. Remove from heat and add lime juice and salt and pepper.

3. Cool soup and puree in a blender or food processor. Serve chilled or warm, garnished with chopped cilantro.

GRILLED SPICY MOROCCAN CHICKEN WITH QUINOA

A SECRET SPRING DINNER *page 68*

6 servings

3 garlic cloves, minced

2 tablespoons minced ginger root

2 tablespoons garam masala

4 tablespoons olive oil

Salt and pepper to taste

6 chicken breasts

1 cup quinoa

Chicken broth

½ cup toasted pine nuts

¼ cup chopped cilantro

1. In a large bowl, mix together garlic, ginger, garam masala, oil, and salt and pepper. Add chicken to marinade and coat thoroughly. Refrigerate for 2 hours.

2. Prepare grill. Cook chicken on medium heat for 8 to 10 minutes on each side.

3. Meanwhile, cook quinoa in chicken broth according to package directions. Fluff with a fork. Add toasted pine nuts. Serve garnished with cilantro.

ASPARAGUS WITH LEMON CONFIT

A SECRET SPRING DINNER *page 68*

6 to 8 servings

3 lemons

1 medium onion, chopped

¼ cup sugar

½ pound asparagus, cut into ½-inch pieces

2 tablespoons chopped parsley

Salt and pepper to taste

1. With a paring knife, remove the zest from the lemons and julienne the zest. Reserve lemons. Put the zest in a small saucepan, cover with water, and boil for 5 minutes. Drain and cool.

2. Remove and discard as much white pith as possible from the peeled lemons; discard pits. Chop lemon flesh.

3. In a small saucepan on medium heat, combine onion, chopped lemons, julienned zest, and sugar. Bring to a boil. Reduce heat to simmer and cook for 5 to 7 minutes.

4. Add asparagus and cook an additional 5 to 7 minutes, until mixture thickens and asparagus are tender. Add salt, pepper, and parsley and serve.

Strawberry Pavlova A Secret Spring Dinner *page 68*

This recipe first appears in The Camellia Dinner. See page 79 for the recipe.

ZUCCHINI AND WATERCRESS SOUP

AN AL FRESCO LUNCH *page 76*

8 servings

4 tablespoons butter

1 cup minced shallots

3 garlic cloves, coarsely chopped

3 medium potatoes, peeled and cubed

6 cups chicken broth

2 pounds zucchini, coarsely chopped

4 loosely packed cups watercress (leaves and small stems)

Salt and freshly ground pepper to taste

Pinch of cayenne

1. Melt butter in a soup pot and add shallots, garlic, and potatoes, and sauté over medium heat for 5 minutes. Add chicken broth and simmer until potatoes are cooked, about 10 minutes.

2. Add zucchini and cook for 10 minutes. Remove from heat and add watercress. Let watercress wilt for 5 minutes. Puree in the bowl of a food processor or blender. Add more broth, if needed, to puree to desired thickness.

3. Add salt, pepper, and cayenne to taste. Serve chilled or hot.

WHITE BEAN AND SHRIMP SALAD

AN AL FRESCO LUNCH *page 76*

6 servings

3 cups cooked white beans

¾ cup diced celery

¾ cup diced red onion

1 large garlic clove, minced

1½ pounds medium shrimp, cooked

¼ cup olive oil

Juice and zest of 1 medium lemon

1 teaspoon fresh thyme, or ½ teaspoon dried

1 teaspoon fresh oregano, or ½ teaspoon dried

½ cup chopped parsley

Salt and freshly ground pepper to taste

1 pint cherry tomatoes, halved

Spinach or lettuce

1. Combine all of the ingredients except for tomatoes. Let ingredients marinate for 1 hour.

2. Fold in tomatoes and serve atop greens.

COCONUT CAKE

AN AL FRESCO LUNCH *page 76*

Makes one 9-inch 2-layer cake

2¼ cups sifted cake flour

2½ teaspoons baking powder

½ teaspoon salt

1¼ cups sugar

1 stick butter

2 cups unsweetened coconut milk

1 teaspoon vanilla

2 cups shredded coconut

1 tablespoon grated lemon zest, plus ½ teaspoon

4 large egg whites, beaten, plus 1 large egg white
 for frosting

2 cups heavy cream

3 tablespoons sugar

3 cups flaked coconut

1. Preheat oven to 350° F. Butter and flour two 9-inch cake pans. Resift flour with baking powder and salt.

2. Beat together the sugar and butter until fluffy. In a separate bowl, combine coconut milk and vanilla.

3. Add sifted ingredients to the butter mixture in three parts, alternating with a third of the coconut milk mixture each time. Beat after each addition until smooth.

4. Stir in coconut and 1 tablespoon lemon zest. Gently fold the 4 beaten egg whites into batter. Pour batter into prepared cake pans and bake for 25 minutes or until a tester inserted into the middle comes out clean. Cool cakes on a rack. Remove from pan.

5. To make the frosting, whip cream, 1 egg white, sugar, and ½ teaspoon lemon zest until peaks form. Ice layers and sides of cake and cover with the flaked coconut.

THE KEY TO A FLUFFY BUT DURABLE ICING: WHIPPED EGG WHITE KEEPS THE CREAM ICING FROM MELTING AND HELPS THE COCONUT ADHERE TO THE CAKE.

SUMMER

Summer brings an em
riches. The heady sce
of homegrown tomat
expression of annual
heat of the midday su
me with delight. Onc
the perennial borders
vegetable and cutting
kitchen, the tabletops

barrassment of sensual

t of roses, the tang

es, the vibrant

owers, even the white

scalding my skin, fill

the flush fades from

in midseason, the

gardens take over the

. . . and my life.

1

A Cascade of Pink at

THE 'CONSTANCE SPRY' LUNCH

In mid-June the six 'Constance Spry' ramblers that cover my studio finally come into bloom. For three weeks, and only three weeks, the shell-pink blossoms, supported by a twelve-foot-tall pergola, smother the studio deck with their delicate color and heady scent. It is too magnificent a spectacle not to share. I planned an early lunch so that my guests could catch the roses' scent released by the warm summer sun, and dressed the table to echo the roses: a palette of celadon, pale pink, and white. Each place setting was defined with a silver beaker of roses, unripe blueberries, and a few tails of small-leafed variegated ivy. As I served lunch, I realized that much of the food reflected the same color scheme, from the pale green cucumber soup to the herbed mayonnaise to the pomegranate ice cream. All unplanned. Sometimes things really just do happen perfectly.

A trio of roses at their peak blush while the etched Venetian glass dazzles.

LITTLE

original invention was necessary to create this feminine table. The voluptuous roses decided the color scheme for me, as they dictated the placement of the table next to the flush pergola. Following Constance's lead, I chose pink and green transferware plates, pale green Venetian crystal, and a sage matelassé tablecloth. Individual miniature bouquets—nestled in inexpensive silver plate mint julep cups—echo the larger bouquet and extend the centerpiece out onto the table. Unadorned Christofle silver plate flatware and plain white linen pullwork napkins do not distract from the starring player.

Weeping Branches Create

AN OUTDOOR DINING ROOM

When I was small, I loved making a secret house, like most children, under the droopy branches of a weeping willow. The canopy formed from the branches of a pair of weeping birches brought back those childhood idylls and was a natural inspiration for creating a magical outdoor dining room. I brought out my prized made-to-order faïence plates, manufactured by the same French factory that produced them in the eighteenth century. I still marvel at the hand-painted botanical designs, and the two-tone leaf pattern that borders each plate. Not to distract from the plates' uniqueness, I used a white cloth, made from two matelassé bedspreads, and white linen napkins. Since I love to mix formal and rustic, I added stressed-green-painted outdoor chairs and topped the table with branches of white dogwood and mountain laurel.

the *Menu*

ASPARAGUS WRAPPED IN VEAL AND STRAWBERRY RHUBARB SORBET (ABOVE LEFT AND RIGHT) ATOP HAND-PAINTED FAÏENCE PLATES (LEFT) MAKE AN ELEGANT STATEMENT, EVEN WHEN PAIRED WITH A SIMPLE RUSTIC BOUQUET OF MOUNTAIN LAUREL AND DOGWOOD.

Red, White, and Blue Cheer for

INDEPENDENCE DAY

This particular Fourth of July snuck up on me. I was too consumed with obsessive puttering in the garden to give much thought to a holiday theme. So when I found myself with a few hours remaining before guests arrived, I gave up trying to be tricky. I simply let Betsy Ross dictate the day. Once the flag was up, I gathered an assortment of red, white, and blue picnicware that I had collected over the years, and unearthed a simple red checked tablecloth. I cut the first early red zinnias, and used bowls of red fruits in season (cherries and plums from the supermarket) to flank the zinnias. Fortunately, the food was better planned: A flank steak lay marinating in the fridge, the salad was prepared, and I just needed to ice the startling red velvet cake. When we finished the meal and the two bottles of Merlot, the group broke out in a spirited water pistol fight.

the Menu

ONION, AVOCADO, AND TOMATO SALAD

GRILLED FLANK STEAK

SWEET AND WHITE POTATO SALAD
  WITH RASPBERRY VINAIGRETTE

RED VELVET CAKE* & HOMEMADE VANILLA ICE CREAM

FRESH FRUIT

1998 GEYSER PEAK MERLOT, NORTH COAST

Never pass up a good bargain, even out of season. I found the red glass plates on sale for $2.50 each at an after-the-holidays sale. Christmas red easily translates into Independence Day red.

4

Classic Blue and White

AT HOME WITH ROSES

Blue and white is a constant refrain in many of my decorating schemes; I have never found a color that isn't at home with this classic combination. At any price level you can find chic blue and white dishes, vases, and fabrics that are infinitely pleasing to the eye. And although a tabletop of pricey seventeenth-century Kangxi or eighteenth-century Delft china is enviable, a few good antique export pieces buttressed by inexpensive modern reproductions—one of my favorite "cheats"—will serve just as well. The rigid geometrics of bold stripes ground the various patterns of the china, but, most important, allow the color of any roses you choose to leap out brilliantly.

Butter-yellow roses tipped in coral, a collection of David Austin rosy coral roses, a few dusty red roses, and unripe blueberries come to life on a platform of blue and white.

Carrot Leek Soup with Orange Essence*

Paillard of Chicken Sautéed in Sherry on a Bed of
  Fresh Mixed Greens

Fraise des Bois with Crème Frâiche

1999 Yamhill Valley Vineyards Pinot Blanc,
  Willamette Valley

Evoking Tuscany with a

GREENHOUSE IDYLL

When June warms up enough to guarantee mild evening temper-
atures, I move the potted citrus and camellia trees out of the
greenhouse—a relief from waves of winter whitefly, scale, and
aphid abuse—into the clean summer air. When I see the few
plants clustered against the whitewashed greenhouse walls, I am
reminded of al fresco dinners in the Tuscan countryside, and
decide to re-create the scene for dinner guests. A raffia tablecloth
and green pottery plates from Provence (not Tuscan, but close
enough) seem fitting with wicker-covered glasses and bamboo-
handled flatware. A few clipped boughs of olive and citrus made
a quick centerpiece, but since I am unwilling to sacrifice my own
trees, I import the lemon-laden branches from the flower market.

the Menu

Chilled Watercress Soup

Lemon-Dill Pasta Salad with Shrimp and Grapes*

Salad of Mixed Baby Greens with Fig Vinaigrette

Assortment of Olives

Crusty Rustic Bread

Lemon Meringue Pie

1998 Luna Pinot Grigio, Napa Valley

Carnations and Cakes Say

HAPPY BIRTHDAY

In mid-July I offered to give a friend a birthday party, but I was stuck with two weeks of downtime in the garden: The roses and perennials were spent, and the cutting garden hadn't begun to produce flowers. I fell back on my favorite blue-and-white combo for inspiration, but I wanted a more streamlined, modern atmosphere than I'd created with the same theme earlier in the summer. As I often do when looking for a sleek line, I chose carnations for the centerpiece. There is something about the rigid form of the flower, coupled with its contrary raggedy edge, that gives it a contemporary air when massed . . . that, plus carnations were available and cheap. I chose plain blue rectangular pots to play off the rounded dome of white carnations, and a simple striped tablecloth to bring in some vertical lines. To carry the theme further—this was no frilly Queen Anne's lace kind of birthday girl—I wrapped the packages in solids and stripes, but interrupted the tight theme with one Mod floral package. To flow the flowers out onto the table, I tucked blossoms of carnation and daisy—another modern flower— under the blue cotton bows. Fortunately, I finished the table before the martinis arrived.

WHEN dressing a table, I always try to repeat a smaller decorative element, thereby extending its impact. The daisies on the cakes (opposite) were echoed on the package (below), as the stripes on the tablecloth are repeated on the wrapping paper. To keep the flowers fresh, I tuck them under the ribbon at the last moment, or push them into a floral water vial, hiding the base of the vial with a plump bow.

When in doubt, keep it simple: Crisp stripes and solids in summery shades of blue make a stunning impact.

the *Menu*

Vichyssoise

Swordfish Beurre Blanc

Roasted Mixed Vegetables with Orzo

Mixed Salad

Daire's Fudgy Rum Chocolate Cake*

Grey Goose Vodka Martinis

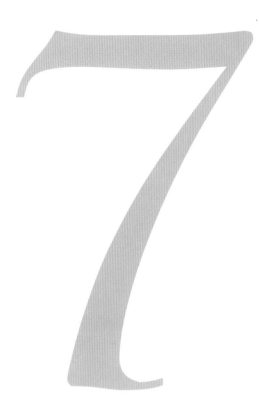

Nautical Themes at

A Lobster Feast

To escape the Midwest, my mother and aunt make an annual summer pilgrimage to Connecticut. The sisters say they make the trip to see my gardens at their peak, but I'm not so sure. I think the real reason for their trek is to get closer to the source of fresh lobster. I may be three hours away from the nearest crustacean habitat, but that proximity seems enough of a lure to my mother and aunt. My aunt's birthday coincides with her visit, and it has become a tradition to celebrate with a lobster dinner. For best size and flavor we selected 1½- to 2-pound lobsters, and to accompany the sweet white meat, I make crispy paper-thin onion rings. (The secret recipe was diplomatically wheedled out of a chef at a California roadside restaurant.) I had bought the nautical restaurantware plates for $1 apiece from a club that was going out of business and paired them with inexpensive Polish cobalt glass. An instantaneous transplant of bold red geraniums from plastic pot to terra-cotta finished the scene.

WE dragged the rustic kitchen table outside to take advantage of the fine weather, followed by my dog Pookie (who never complains when called on to serve as a prop). The rather formal dining chairs take on a more playful air when upholstered in red checked cotton and paired with the simple farm table.

the Menu

STEAMED LOBSTERS

CALIFORNIA FRIED ONION RINGS*

OLD-FASHIONED BAKED BEANS

SLICED TOMATOES AND ONIONS WITH CHOPPED BASIL

ANGEL FOOD CAKE WITH SLICED PEACHES

 AND WHIPPED CREAM

1998. SAPPHIRE HILL CHARDONNAY,

 RUSSIAN RIVER VALLEY

the Menu

THE TAIL OF STEAMED SPICY LOBSTER PAIRED WITH CRISPY THIN FRIED ONION RINGS AND BAKED BEANS SERVED ON HEAVY CHINA RESTAURANTWARE AND BISTRO FLATWARE.

8

A Reflection on Cool Whites

DINNER BY THE POOL

Having spent childhood in the Midwest deprived of ocean, I've over-compensated as an adult by trying to spend as much summer indulgence time as possible near water. Since I don't have a house near the sea, and can't bear to vacation when the Weatherstone gardens are flush, I try to entertain near the sound of the pond cascade, or by the quiet stillness of the pool. I surround the gray slate pool with white potted rose standards and agapanthas (note to self: After seven years, isn't it time to repot the agapanthas?) and repeat the flowers, filling in with white carnations, in the centerpiece. Nothing more is needed to adorn the minimalist atmosphere other than a navy blue raffia tablecloth, plain white plates, well-starched white napkins, and simple ceramic serving pieces.

the Menu

Smoky Cumin Chicken*

Rigatoni with Summer Vegetables*

Mesclun Salad with Basil Vinaigrette

Blueberry Rhubarb Pie*

1998 La Millière Côtes du Rhône
Rouge Vieilles Vignes, Rhône Valley

FOR the past seven summers, the fourteen potted white agapanthas and five rose standards have moved from their winter digs in the greenhouse to line the rim of the pool. The wisteria-covered pergola provides refuge from the summer sun and hides a simple dining table suitable for midday and evening dining.

The juice and zest of an orange intensify the flavors of blueberry and rhubarb.

Made in the Shade

A PONDSIDE PICNIC

Having attended one too many formal dinners in my life, I am always happiest when I come back down to the ground. On this crystalline summer day, the cotton may not have been high, but the fish were jumping out of the pond. I had a craving for fried chicken and dappled shade. I gathered a collection of baskets and filled them with fruit, cheese, bread, cherry tomatoes, an armful of hydrangeas, and the fresh fried chicken. A trip to the greenhouse shed produced four bamboo stakes to which I attached a blue-and-white checked length of diaphanous voile, and held down the fabric with raffia. Canopy completed, I spread out the tablecloth and plumped the gingham pillows. After devouring the movable feast, I threw a few heels of bread at the pond carp and settled down with my book. Two pages later, I was sound asleep.

the *Menu*

Weatherstone Fried Chicken*

Green Bean Vinaigrette

Mixed Green Salad

Assortment of Fruits and Cheeses

Freshly Baked Baguettes

Three-Berry Pie*

1998 Martinborough Vineyard Chardonnay

*Vivid blue hydrangeas accompany baskets filled with three-berry pie,
spicy fried chicken, and fresh baked bread.*

Variations on a Theme

MORE BLUE AND WHITE

My obsession with blue and white encompasses not just export china, English transferware, and table linens, but also etched crystal and cobalt glass. I have collected all of these for the past thirty years, mixing discount-store glass with treasured antique porcelain. If I run out of ideas, or if time constraints hover, I can fall back on that collection for a quick mix-and-match tabletop. Since my stash is spotty in parts, I use that to my advantage. I mix glass patterns, just as I mix patterns of dinner service to create a more interesting and less static table. Of course, picking a common denominator—all Chinese patterns, or all English transfer ware, or all bird patterns—harmonizes the collection. To center the eye, I add a spot of color: The jumble of roses, or any mixed bouquet, looks focused against a cool background of blue and white. To add vertical structure to the arrangement, I flank the central bouquet with faux miniature boxwood topiaries.

Creating a Romance with

A Floating Picnic

I have a small pond dotted with a miniature island flanked by two old ash trees. I used to row a lawn mower over to the island to cut the grass, but soon gave up. Better, I decided, to let the island go wild with loosestrife, Queen Anne's lace, black-eyed Susans, daisies, and, later in the summer, goldenrod. Although the idea was born from laziness, it turned out to be an excellent decision. The wildflower island looks like a well-planned bouquet in the middle of the pond and is of interest all season long. I like to row the canoe, packed with picnic baskets loaded with food, out to the Lilliputian island and have a lazy afternoon watching the carp jump out of the water as they snatch a less appetizing lunch of gnats and flies.

A collection of wildflowers (Queen Anne's lace, black-eyed Susans, and daisies), supported by domesticated posies (nepeta, cosmos, and monarda) from the cutting garden, stand out atop a red-and-white checked bistro tablecloth (opposite). Wicker baskets and matching paper plate holders coupled with fiery red tin containers (below) contain the portable feast.

Picnic essentials: plastic flatware and cups, cookie tins, bistro cloth, and wicker baskets

The picnic packed and stored in the canoe,
we are ready to push off to the mini-isle for
a lazy day of fish watching.

Coleslaw flecked with almonds, grilled baby back ribs, and a simple salad of pesto-tossed fresh mozzarella and cherry tomatoes from the garden garnished with a sprig of basil (below). The final indulgence: Chocolate Pecan Pie Bars (opposite).

the Menu

Barbecued Baby Back Ribs*

Jeanne's Asian Coleslaw*

Fresh Mozzarella, Tomato, and Pesto Salad*

Crudités of Radish, Olives, Scallions

Baker's® Chocolate Pecan Pie Bars*

Collection of Imported Beers

Cobalt and Yellow Pair for
A SEAFOOD LUNCHEON

When late summer comes to Connecticut, I turn to the cutting garden—sowed in croplike rows of unfashionable flowers such as zinnia, marigolds, and tickseed: Crayola yellows and blatant oranges dominate. Their lack of subtlety, which irks fussy gardening purists, along with their cheerful willingness to bloom nonstop, suits me fine. In August, when everything else in the garden looks bedraggled, I am grateful that my common annuals proliferate. And what better way to show them off than to skip to the opposite side of the color wheel, straight to cobalt blue? It must be the contrarian in me, but when flower snobs dictate what's chic and what's not (carnations, for example), I fight back with big bouquets and attitude.

Marigold 'Climax'

Zinnia 'Canary Bird'

Sunflower 'Sonia'

Sunflower 'Valentine'

Coreopsis 'Bright Lights'

Zinnia 'Tetra Mix' Orange

Sunflower 'Pacino'

Rudbeckia 'Indian Summer'

Coreopsis tinctoria

the Menu

MELON AND PROSCIUTTO WITH LIME

SEAFOOD EN PAPILLOTE*

ARUGULA SALAD WITH SHAVED PARMESAN

LEMON SORBET IN LEMON CUPS

PEACH SORBET IN PEACH CUPS

1997 D'AQUINO GAVI DI GAVI, PIEDMONT

ASPARAGUS, VEAL, AND PROSCIUTTO BUNDLES

AN OUTDOOR DINING ROOM *page 105*

6 to 8 servings

32 asparagus stalks

8 slices veal scaloppine (18 ounces)

8 thin slices prosciutto

¼ cup all-purpose flour

2 tablespoons unsalted butter

3 tablespoons olive oil

4 large shallots, chopped

1 pound mushrooms, sliced

½ cup dry white wine

1 cup rich chicken or veal broth

½ cup heavy cream

Salt and pepper to taste

1. Clean and trim asparagus, discarding woody stems. Tips should be 4 inches in length. Steam until slightly tender, or immerse in boiling water for about 3 minutes. After boiling, drain, rinse under cold running water, and let cool.

2. Pound veal slices until ¼ inch thick. Place a slice of prosciutto on top of each veal scallop. Place 4 asparagus tips at one end of each veal scallop, roll up meat, and secure with a toothpick.

3. Dredge each bundle in flour and shake off excess.

4. Heat butter and olive oil in a large frying pan over medium-high heat. Sauté scaloppine bundles quickly to brown all over, about 2 minutes. Remove and stack on a plate; cover with foil to keep warm.

5. In the same pan on medium-high heat, sauté shallots for 2 minutes. Add mushrooms and sauté another 5 minutes. Add white wine and boil 1 minute, scraping up bits from bottom of the pan.

6. Add chicken broth and cream and lower heat. Simmer 5 minutes. Season with salt and pepper. Add asparagus bundles and simmer, turning with tongs until heated through, about 2 minutes. Remove toothpicks and serve immediately.

Option: Serve with extra asparagus and jasmine rice to soak up the sauce.

STRAWBERRY RHUBARB SORBET

AN OUTDOOR DINING ROOM *page 105*

8 to 10 servings (about 6 cups)

1 cup sugar

1 cup water

1½ cups rhubarb chopped in ½-inch pieces

1 pint strawberries, washed, stemmed, and halved

1 teaspoon lemon juice

1. Combine all ingredients in a medium saucepan and simmer, partially covered, for 15 minutes, until fruit is very soft. Cool and refrigerate until chilled.

2. Process the mixture in an ice cream maker and freeze.

RED VELVET CAKE

INDEPENDENCE DAY *page 108*

Makes one 8-inch 2-layer cake

2 sticks butter

1½ cups sugar, plus 1 cup for icing

2 large eggs

2 ounces red food coloring

2 tablespoons cocoa

¼ teaspoon salt

1 cup buttermilk

2¼ cups sifted cake flour

2 teaspoons vanilla extract

1 teaspoon baking soda

1 tablespoon vinegar

One 8-ounce package of cream cheese

1 box confectioners' sugar

1. Preheat oven to 350° F. Grease and flour two 8-inch round pans. With an electric mixer, cream 1 stick of butter with 1½ cups sugar. Add eggs one at a time and beat well after each addition.

2. Make a paste of food coloring, cocoa, and salt and add to mixture. Add buttermilk, alternating with flour in thirds. Add 1 teaspoon vanilla extract. Dissolve soda in vinegar and stir into batter, blending all ingredients as little as possible.

3. Pour batter into prepared pans and bake for 35 to 40 minutes or until a tester inserted in middle comes out clean. Cool cakes on a wire rack.

4. Beat the remaining stick of butter and the cream cheese together. Gradually add confectioners' sugar and remaining vanilla. Beat until smooth. Ice the tops of both cake halves, then stack and ice sides.

CARROT LEEK SOUP WITH ORANGE ESSENCE

AT HOME WITH ROSES *page 113*

6 to 8 servings

3 tablespoons olive oil

2 tablespoons butter

2 tablespoons minced ginger

3 medium leeks (white part only),
    cleaned and coarsely chopped

1 cup coarsely chopped shallots

3 stalks celery, coarsely chopped

One 2-pound bag peeled baby carrots

6 cups chicken broth

Zest and juice of 1 orange

1 teaspoon salt

½ teaspoon white pepper

1. In a large soup pot heat olive oil and butter until butter melts. Add ginger, leeks, shallots, and celery, and sauté until translucent. Add carrots and cook for 2 more minutes.

2. Add chicken broth and orange zest and juice, and cook until carrots are tender, about 15 minutes.

3. Cool soup slightly. Add salt and pepper. Puree in an immersion blender or food processor. Reheat and serve.

LEMON-DILL PASTA SALAD WITH SHRIMP AND GRAPES

GREENHOUSE IDYLL *page 116*

6 servings

1 pound farfalle, radiatori, or any medium-size pasta

2 pounds large shrimp

2 tablespoons plus ½ cup olive oil

Salt and freshly ground pepper to taste

2 garlic cloves, coarsely chopped

Juice of 1 lemon (about 4 tablespoons)

½ cup coarsely chopped dill

1 pound red grapes, washed and stemmed

1. Cook pasta al dente according to package directions. Rinse and drain.

2. Clean, peel, and devein shrimp. In a large frying pan, heat 2 tablespoons of olive oil. Sauté shrimp for about 4 minutes, or until pink, and season with salt and pepper.

3. In a food processor, combine garlic, lemon juice, and dill. Add ½ cup olive oil in a slow stream while processing. Continue to process until an emulsion forms.

4. Combine pasta, shrimp, and grapes in a large bowl and toss with dressing. Readjust seasonings. Serve at room temperature.

IF YOU USE LARGE GRAPES IN THE PASTA SALAD (LEFT), THEY CAN BE HALVED. THE QUALITY OF THE CAKE ICING (RIGHT) DEPENDS ON THE PERCENTAGE OF COCOA IN THE BAKING CHOCOLATE: 70 PERCENT IS RECOMMENDED.

DAIRE'S FUDGY RUM CHOCOLATE CAKE

HAPPY BIRTHDAY *page 121*

**Makes one 10-inch Bundt cake
or 6 individual cakes**

8 ounces unsweetened chocolate

2 teaspoons instant coffee

2 teaspoons rum

2 tablespoons boiling water

4 eggs

2 teaspoons vanilla

2 cups confectioners' sugar

2 tablespoons arrowroot

3 cups heavy cream

16 ounces bittersweet chocolate

1. Preheat oven to 350° F. In a small saucepan over low heat, melt unsweetened chocolate. Cool slightly and add coffee, rum, and water.

2. In a separate bowl, beat together eggs, vanilla, sugar, and arrowroot with an electric mixer. Beat until doubled in bulk.

3. In a second bowl, whip 1 cup of cream with the mixer until peaks form. Add chocolate mixture to egg mixture and fold in cream.

4. Pour batter into a greased and floured Bundt pan and bake for 1 hour (20 minutes for mini Bundt cakes) or until tester comes out clean. Cool cake completely before icing with ganache.

5. In a medium saucepan over low heat, melt bittersweet chocolate and remaining cream, stirring constantly. When chocolate is melted and smooth, cool slightly and pour over cakes.

CALIFORNIA FRIED ONION RINGS

A LOBSTER FEAST *page 126*

6 to 8 servings

1 cup flour

2 tablespoons sugar

½ teaspoon cayenne pepper

2 teaspoons chili powder

1 tablespoon salt

2 large Spanish onions

Vegetable oil for deep-frying

1. In a glass roasting pan mix flour, sugar, cayenne, chili powder, and salt.

2. Slice onions very thinly, using a mandoline, if possible.

3. Add 2 inches of vegetable oil to a deep skillet. Heat oil over medium-high heat until a drop of water sizzles.

4. Separate sliced onions and add to spiced flour in batches, shaking off excess flour.

5. Deep-fry in the oil in batches until golden brown. Drain on paper towels and serve immediately.

RIGATONI WITH SUMMER VEGETABLES

DINNER BY THE POOL *page 130*

8 servings

2 cups fresh corn (from about 4 ears)

1 each small red, yellow, and orange pepper,
coarsely chopped

1 jalapeño pepper, minced

4 medium zucchini, sliced

1 large red onion, coarsely chopped

2 cups cherry tomatoes, halved

Salt and freshly ground pepper to taste

¼ cup plus 2 tablespoons olive oil

1 pound rigatoni, cooked and drained

2 garlic cloves, minced

1 cup chicken broth

Juice and zest of 1 lime, lemon,
and orange

2 teaspoons honey

¼ cup coarsely chopped cilantro

¼ cup fresh basil, cut into chiffonade

1. Preheat oven to 400° F. In a roasting pan, place the corn, peppers, zucchini, onion, tomatoes, salt, pepper, and ¼ cup oil. Toss well and roast for 20 minutes or until vegetables are tender. Add vegetables to pasta and mix well.

2. In a small saucepan, sauté garlic in 2 tablespoons oil for 1 minute. Add chicken broth, citrus juices, and honey, and reduce by half.

3. Pour stock-citrus sauce over pasta. Add cilantro and basil and toss pasta well. Correct seasonings and serve at room temperature, garnished with citrus zest.

AROMATIC CUMIN GIVES A MEDITERRANEAN TOUCH TO AN AMERICAN SUMMER STAPLE (LEFT). NANCY CONTINUES TO INVENT MOUTH-WATERING WAYS TO ABSORB THE GARDEN SURPLUS, SUCH AS THE ROASTED VEGETABLE PASTA (RIGHT).

SMOKY CUMIN CHICKEN

DINNER BY THE POOL   *page 130*

8 servings

1 small onion, finely diced

4 garlic cloves, minced

2 tablespoons ground cumin

1 teaspoon ground chipotle pepper

2 tablespoons chili powder

3 tablespoons honey

2 tablespoons Dijon mustard

4 tablespoons Worcestershire sauce

½ cup ketchup

¼ cup olive oil

Two 2½-to-3-pound whole chickens, each cut into 8 pieces

1. Mix together all the ingredients except the chicken. Thoroughly coat the chicken pieces with the marinade. Refrigerate for at least 1 hour or up to 24 hours.

2. Prepare a grill or preheat the oven to 350° F. Grill, turning once, or bake the chicken for 35 minutes or until cooked through.

BLUEBERRY RHUBARB PIE

DINNER BY THE POOL   *page 130*

Makes one 10-inch pie

1 Basic Tart Dough recipe (see below)

2 cups blueberries

2 cups rhubarb, cut into 1-inch pieces

¼ cup flour

½ cup sugar

¼ cup honey

¼ cup freshly squeezed orange juice

¼ cup freshly squeezed lemon juice

2 tablespoons orange zest

2 tablespoons lemon zest

2 tablespoons butter

1. Preheat oven to 400° F. Make the dough and set aside. Place berries and rhubarb in a large bowl. Sprinkle with flour and sugar, toss well to coat, then add honey, orange and lemon juice and zest, and toss again.

2. Roll out half the dough. Fit into the bottom of a 9-inch pie plate. Pour in the filling and dot with butter.

3. Roll out remaining dough and place on top of pie; crimp the edges. Bake for 15 minutes, then reduce heat to 350° F and bake for 40 minutes or until crust is browned. Cool and serve at room temperature.

Basic Tart Dough

2½ cups flour

2 sticks unsalted butter, chilled and cut into small dice

Pinch of salt

3 to 4 tablespoons ice water

1. Put flour and salt into the bowl of a food processor and pulse 3 times to blend. Add butter, and pulse processor about 8 times to cut in butter. Dough should resemble coarse cornmeal and butter pieces should be no larger than small peas.

2. Add ice water gradually by tablespoons through the feed tube while pulsing machine. Dough will begin to come together in a ball.

3. Remove dough from processor, shape into a disk, sprinkle lightly with flour, and wrap in wax paper. Refrigerate until ready to roll out.

WEATHERSTONE FRIED CHICKEN

A PONDSIDE PICNIC   *page 137*

6 servings

6 garlic cloves, peeled and cut in half

3 bay leaves, torn into pieces

1 tablespoon ground Hungarian paprika

¼ cup olive oil

4 tablespoons red wine vinegar

4 tablespoons lemon juice

1 teaspoon cayenne pepper

Salt and freshly ground pepper to taste

1 whole fryer chicken, cut into 8 pieces

½ cup flour

¼ cup peanut oil

1. In a large bowl, whisk together the garlic, bay leaves, paprika, olive oil, vinegar, lemon juice, cayenne, and salt and pepper.

2. Add chicken pieces to marinade and coat well. Cover and let chicken marinate in the refrigerator for 24 hours, turning 3 or 4 times.

3. Dredge chicken in flour, shaking off excess.

4. Heat oil in a large skillet under medium-high flame. Add chicken pieces and fry (in batches if necessary) about 10 minutes on each side, or until brown and crispy. Drain on paper towels or brown paper. Serve warm.

THREE-BERRY PIE

A PONDSIDE PICNIC   *page 137*

Makes one 9-inch pie

1 Basic Tart Dough Recipe (see page 159)

1½ pints blueberries

1 pint blackberries

1 pint raspberries

1 cup sugar plus 2 tablespoons

juice and grated zest of 1 orange

¼ cup quick tapioca

1 large egg, beaten

1. Preheat oven to 400° F. Roll out half the dough and place in the bottom of a 9-inch pie plate.

2. In a large bowl, gently mix the berries, 1 cup sugar, orange juice, zest, and tapioca. Let rest for 10 minutes, then put berries on bottom crust.

3. Roll out remaining dough and place on top of the pie. Crimp and cut the edges, then brush the top with egg. Sprinkle with 2 tablespoons sugar.

4. Bake for 45 minutes or until golden brown.

BARBECUED BABY BACK RIBS

A FLOATING PICNIC *page 149*

6 servings

1 small onion, minced

2 garlic cloves, minced

1 teaspoon dried Thai chile peppers, crushed

½ cup soy sauce

4 tablespoons tomato paste

¼ cup honey

¼ cup apple cider vinegar

¼ cup olive oil

3 pounds baby back ribs

1. In a blender or food processor, combine the onion, garlic, chile peppers, soy sauce, tomato paste, honey, vinegar, and olive oil. Generously coat the ribs with the sauce.
2. Prepare the grill. Cook ribs on very low heat for 30 to 40 minutes on each side. Serve immediately.

JEANNE'S ASIAN COLESLAW

A FLOATING PICNIC *page 149*

8 servings

One 3-pound cabbage, shredded

3 bunches scallions, sliced

Salt and pepper to taste

1 package ramen noodles, uncooked and crumbled

⅓ cup rice vinegar

⅓ cup sugar

1 cup slivered almonds

4 tablespoons butter

⅔ cup olive oil

1. Mix cabbage, scallions, salt and pepper, and ramen noodles.
2. Add vinegar and sugar and toss well.
3. Sauté almonds in butter until just browned. Just before serving, add almonds and olive oil.

Fresh Mozzarella, Tomato, and Pesto Salad

A FLOATING PICNIC *page 149*

6 servings
¼ cup pine nuts, toasted
2 garlic cloves
1 cup chopped basil
4 tablespoons olive oil

3 tablespoons grated Parmigiano-Reggiano cheese
Salt and freshly ground pepper to taste
2 pounds fresh mozzarella cheese
5 large tomatoes, or 1 pint cherry tomatoes

1. With a mortar and pestle, mash the pine nuts, garlic, and basil into a paste. Add olive oil and stir until smooth. Add Parmigiano-Reggiano and mix well. Add salt and pepper to taste and set aside.
2. Slice mozzarella and tomatoes into ¼-inch-thick rounds and fan out alternately on a serving plate or platter. (If using cherry tomatoes, cube mozzarella.)
3. Drizzle tomatoes and mozzarella with pesto and serve.

Baker's® Chocolate Pecan Pie Bars

A FLOATING PICNIC *page 149*

Makes 48 bars
2 cups flour
2 cups sugar
2 sticks butter, softened
¼ teaspoon salt

1½ cups light corn syrup
6 squares Baker's® semisweet baking chocolate
4 eggs, slightly beaten
1½ teaspoons vanilla
2½ cups chopped pecans

1. Preheat oven to 350° F. Grease the bottom and sides of a 15 x 10-inch baking pan. In a large bowl, with mixer at medium speed, beat the flour, ½ cup sugar, butter, and salt until mixture resembles coarse crumbs. Press firmly and evenly into prepared baking pan. Bake for 20 minutes or until lightly browned.
2. Meanwhile, in a 3-quart saucepan, combine corn syrup and chocolate over low heat, stirring constantly, just until chocolate melts. Remove from heat. Stir in remaining sugar, then eggs and vanilla, until blended. Stir in pecans.
3. Pour filling over hot crust and spread evenly. Bake for 35 minutes, or until filling is firm around the edges and slightly soft in the center. Cool in pan on a wire rack.

Baker's® is a registered trademark of KF Holdings.

SEAFOOD EN PAPILLOTE

A SEAFOOD LUNCHEON *page 153*

8 servings

8 garlic cloves, minced

¼ cup olive oil

2 lemons, peeled, zest finely chopped, plus juice of 1 lemon

1 cup chopped parsley

1 cup white wine

2 pounds mussels, cleaned

2 pounds clams, cleaned

1 large onion, diced

Three 28-ounce cans whole peeled tomatoes

2 tablespoons salt

1 tablespoon sugar

1 cup basil, cut into chiffonade

1 teaspoon red pepper flakes

2 pounds spaghetti

Parchment paper

2 pounds large shrimp, peeled and deveined

3 cups cooked lobster meat

1. Preheat oven to 375° F. In a deep skillet on medium heat, sauté garlic in 2 tablespoons olive oil for 2 minutes. Add lemon zest, lemon juice, parsley, and wine and simmer for 2 minutes.

2. Add mussels and clams and cover pan with a tight-fitting lid, shaking pan to ensure even heat. Steam until mussels and clams just open.

3. Remove mussels and clams from the sauce and set them aside. Reduce broth by half.

4. Prepare the marinara: In a large saucepan, sauté onion over medium-high heat until translucent. Crush the tomatoes with your hands and add to pot. Add salt, sugar, basil, and red pepper flakes, and simmer for 20 minutes. Add half the reduced broth from clams and mussels.

5. In a large pot of boiling water, cook spaghetti for half the time recommended. Drain and toss in half the reduced broth.

6. Cut the parchment paper into eight 8- by 12-inch pieces. In the middle of each piece, place 1¼ cups of cooked pasta, then divide clams, mussels, raw shrimp, and lobster among the 8 pieces of parchment paper. Top with a large spoonful of the sauce.

7. Holding the two long sides, fold and crease the top two or three times, keeping the package tight, and twist the ends. Place on a baking sheet and bake for 10 to 12 minutes. Serve immediately in parchment.

THE SWEETEST AND MOST TENDER LOBSTERS WEIGH LESS THAN 1½ POUNDS. LOBSTER DIPPING BUTTER CAN BE IMPROVED WITH A SQUEEZE OF A LEMON, A PINCH OF CAYENNE, AND A SPRINKLE OF CHOPPED PARSLEY.

AUTUMN

Autumn's first frost b
the days of dormancy
harvest continues una
abundance of fruit do
and tabletops. Shorte
frenzy of bulb plantin
of turning leaves. Oc
sunlight spurs a chang
palette: Earthy browr
and soft golds now co

asts the garden;
begin. The apple
ffected and an
minates the kitchen
ned days prompt a
g beneath the boughs
er and orange
e in mood and
s, rusts, wine reds,
ntrol the scene.

1. A Cottage Buffet   2. A Luncheon Getaway   3. Supper in the Country

7. A Weatherstone Dinner   8. A Columbus Day Luncheon   9. Guy Fawkes Day

Bill Blass Joins

A COTTAGE BUFFET

Bill Blass, the clothing designer, teases that I am in constant close touch with my feminine side. I counter with overwhelming evidence of his masculine tastes, evident at his country guest house: animal horns, military and hunting motifs, craggy wood textures, and hewn stone. His notion to merge our tastes for a small buffet lunch produced a pleasing synthesis. I filled grape harvest baskets with boughs of autumn leaves and hydrangeas, then heaped old baskets with apples and wooden bowls with quince. At the center of the bare wood table, I placed a small tub piled with red grapes and two varieties of pear. Individual bouquets of dusty roses (my Yin) peppered with roadside berries nestled in horn cups (his Yang) defined each place setting, adorned with Scottish horn snuffboxes and stag horn flatware. We ate in peaceful harmony.

BORROWING
Bill Blass's masculine lead (and raiding his cupboards), I left the rustic table bare, but dressed it with neo-classical-designed plates, horn-gripped flatware, and bone beakers. Two pairs of glass hurricane lamps shielding beeswax tapers surrounded a centerpiece of fall fruits.

Sparkling wineglasses and hurricane globes reflect the burnished tones of autumn: apple red, dusky yellow, and sepia brown.

the *Menu*

BILL BLASS'S MEAT LOAF

BARBECUED POTATO SKINS WITH CHEDDAR CHEESE

GOLDEN BEET AND ENDIVE SALAD

APPLE CAKE WITH APPLE CIDER GLAZE*

1997 PETERSON WINERY ZINFANDEL,

DRY CREEK VALLEY, AUSTRALIA

A GRAPE HARVEST BASKET (OPPOSITE) HOLDS AN ABUNDANCE OF FALL-TINGED HYDRANGEAS AND VIBURNUM LEAVES. TO REINFORCE THE MASCULINE THEME, A PINECONE CANDLE STANDS AMID THE TEA SERVICE (LEFT). THE OVERFLOW OF APPLES FROM THE ORCHARD RESULTS IN A HARVEST FAVORITE: APPLE BUNDT CAKE (RIGHT).

Autumn Colors Inspire

A LUNCHEON GETAWAY

Sometimes the inspiration for a particular table scene arises from a favorite color scheme, or from a bountiful seasonal vegetable, or from a holiday theme. But at other times, the idea comes from the sheer majesty of a particular place at a singular time. Such was the case for this autumn buffet. It was the waning end of the season. The weatherman had forecast a short run of perfect days ahead: crisp, but sunny and hyperfocused as only the late ocher days of fall can be. I quickly summoned the friendly troops: Join me in an impromptu lunch at a secluded cabin at the end of a nearly inaccessible long dirt road.

THE cabin lacks heating, electricity, and running water, so the food and simple decorations were prepared ahead of time and brought in. The iron stove proved more than adequate for keeping the food and guests warm. I draped the table with plaid picnic blankets and decorated it with 'Jack-Be-Little' pumpkins, hollowed out and filled with dahlias, viburnum berries, and mums swathed in bittersweet.

Celebrate last light of the golden autumn sun with dahlias, mums, and bittersweet.

the Menu

Spicy Pumpkin Seeds

Pâté de Campagne

Game Bird Pot Pie*

Salad of Haricots Verts, Roquefort,
   and Walnuts

Pecan Tarts*

Cheddar Cheese and Grapes

Country Bread Brushed
   with Herbs and Olive Oil

Fresh Apple Cider

1997 Château Pape Clément Bordeaux

A twig basket centerpiece holds gourds from
the garden and a fan of autumn leaves.

THE moon-and-stars motif was repeated on the cheese biscuits (below left), the savory piecrust (below right), and the pecan tarts (opposite). The replication of simple details—textures, colors, shapes, and patterns—gives the table a more cohesive, tailored look. It is always safe to stick to a plain palette and a single botanical, in this case the repetition of maple leaf branches.

A HEARTY GAME BIRD PIE NEEDS NO MORE EMBELLISHMENT THAN A SIMPLE WHITE CASSEROLE DISH. THE PLATES ARE ROYAL WORCESTER'S "HOWARD" PATTERN EDGED IN HUNTER GREEN (ABOVE RIGHT).

A Quiet Sunday Night

SUPPER IN THE COUNTRY

Sunday evening in the country, when the weekenders and guests leave to return to the city, is my evening of rest. I try to plan nothing elaborate on these evenings. Dinner on a tray, or near the kitchen, is all I usually require. I reverse the traditional order of my childhood, when Sunday's dinner was the most formal of the week, and turn to nursery food. The menu of cheddar cheese soup, game hens with dried plum stuffing, and purées of celeriac and winter squash, ending with an almond pear tart, could have been taken from the pages of a Victorian children's novel. I had found a new variety of chrysanthemums over the weekend that would match perfectly with Spode's "Pink Tower" china. The tablecloth, recut from draperies I no longer used, was a medley of all the colors in the dishes, flowers, and food. To keep the simple homey atmosphere, I made small bouquets, which I placed in baskets flanked with wooden candlesticks.

CHRYSANTHEMUM hybridizers keep

inventing new forms and colors. Familiar pompom yellows and oranges give way to shades of burgundy and russet, often tipped or streaked. A majolica pitcher (below) holds a collection of small burnt-rose mums tipped in white, roadside snowberries, and hydrangeas displaying their fall colors. A stuffed poussin, or young chicken (opposite), needs only a small garnish of crab apples.

Glazed English majolica pottery, named after the port in Spain where it originated, enhances the autumnal colors of the bouquet.

the *Menu*

Cheddar Cheese Soup

Game Hens with Dried Plum Stuffing*

Puréed Celariac

Puréed Squash

Almond Pear Tart

1998 Font de Michelle Châteauneuf du Pape

A Formal Fireside

DINNER À DEUX

One day during a muddy September, I decided I needed a lift. Dismissing the chilly wet weather by lighting a fire, I pushed the dining table (I'd call it a dining room table, but I don't have a dining room) in front of the hearth. I pulled out an antique linen tablecloth, the vermeil flatware, the swimming pool–sized Venetian glasses, and the eighteenth-century Imari china, and set a special table for two in front of the fire. Chairs were placed on the same side of the table so we could both stare into the crackling flames. I filled three soup tureens—one large, two miniature—with vibrant dahlias in reds, ranging from the deepest Bordeaux to lacquer and mounded red grapes and plums at the base of the large tureen. As the autumn afternoon faded into dusk, I put on music, stoked the fire, lit the candles, and awaited a romantic evening.

Why save your best for special days? Find an excuse—any will do—to employ treasured linens, crystal, china, and silver.

5

A Haunted Lodge Holds

HALLOWEEN SURPRISES

Although it is difficult for adults to recapture the childhood rapture of Halloween, I try to honor the youthful spirit within all of us on this holiday. According to pagan tradition, which has morphed into modern Halloween, this is the day on which the dead travel to the other world, a day on which the ghosts are able to mingle among the living. And since mingling among the living is one of my favorite occupations, I staged a dinner in an old hunting lodge that the locals say is haunted. I summoned my benevolently spirited friends to huddle around the table and celebrate with a candlelit feast. Whether or not we were successful in warding away the evil spirits, our celebration proved to be a lively one.

A room aglow with the warmth of candlelight creates the perfect setting for the evening's first ghost story. . . .

CELTS used bonfires to aid the dead in their journey from this life to the next as well as to keep the spirits away from the living. A modern-day table filled with cathederal candles acknowledges this tradition, but more practically, adds a warm, festive glow to the celebration. The curving vines of bittersweet and the autumn oak leaves, both roadside finds, are tokens of fall's final harvest.

Candles intertwined with bittersweet vines and autumn oak dance with stars-and-moon pumpkins.

the Menu

GRAVLAX WITH MUSTARD DILL SAUCE

SHORT RIBS WITH SPICY LEMON CAPER SAUCE*

SAUTÉED SPINACH

PARSNIP AND POTATO PURÉE

CRUSTY COUNTRY BREAD

APPLE PEAR CRISP*

TRICK-OR-TREAT CANDY

1998 SANCTUS ST. ÉMILION BORDEAUX GRAND CRU

AN abundant apple harvest from the Weatherstone orchard is always welcome. Those that aren't eaten right off the tree end up in crisps (below) or are mounded high in deep bowls for table decoration. Rustic moss-green glazed-pottery plates complement the artificial bone-handled flatware (opposite) from France. Branches of fall-tinted leaves and 'Jack-Be-Little' minipumpkins complete the orange-and-yellow-hued color theme copied from nature.

6

Relax by the Hearth with

A Small Dinner for Two

When the temperature falls, I turn from being an outdoor garden person to an indoor hearth person. Any hearth will do, even the kitchen stove. Since I am also not a dining room person, I prefer that the table follow my lead. The change of place, change of look, and change of view keeps me cheered during the gray months. A new setting can stimulate the imagination and conversation. This particular dinner was held in a small sitting room off of my bedroom. I threw a cloth over a small table normally stacked high with books and magazines. The colors in the bouquet were chosen to match the screen in the background and pick up the soft red pattern on the chairs. The cranberry hurricanes and glasses complement the flowers and textiles, especially the needlepoint carpet. When setting a table, I always consider the surrounding environment an essential part of the table decor.

try to be mindful of the entire stage—the wall coloring, chairs, paintings, books, carpet—surrounding the table, so that the tabletop flows into and is part of the setting. The Wedgwood pitcher was filled with rose-tinted hydrangeas, dahlias, yarrow, and sedum, then accented with a few small allium to offset the colors in the screen, plates, and fabric.

Consider the room's decorative cues before choosing what to put on your table.

7

A Morning Walk Inspires
A WEATHERSTONE DINNER

Cued by an antique green-and-red paisley Scottish shawl, I gathered seasonal fruits—pomegranates, seckle pears, lady apples, all from the supermarket—for the centerpiece. An afternoon walk in the woods produced the branches of red berries. The bark on the branches made me think of rusted iron—hence the footed urns, which blended with a silver-rimmed wooden bowl staring at me from the cupboard, which echoed the candlesticks. This is how it works sometimes. A painting, a museum postcard, a sliver of wrapping paper, even the produce section, becomes the inspiration for creating the look of the table. Once the spark fires my brain, all the bits and pieces naturally tumble into place. Trust your eye and follow your instincts. Thematic clues are all around you, and some, like dormant winter branches, are free for the taking.

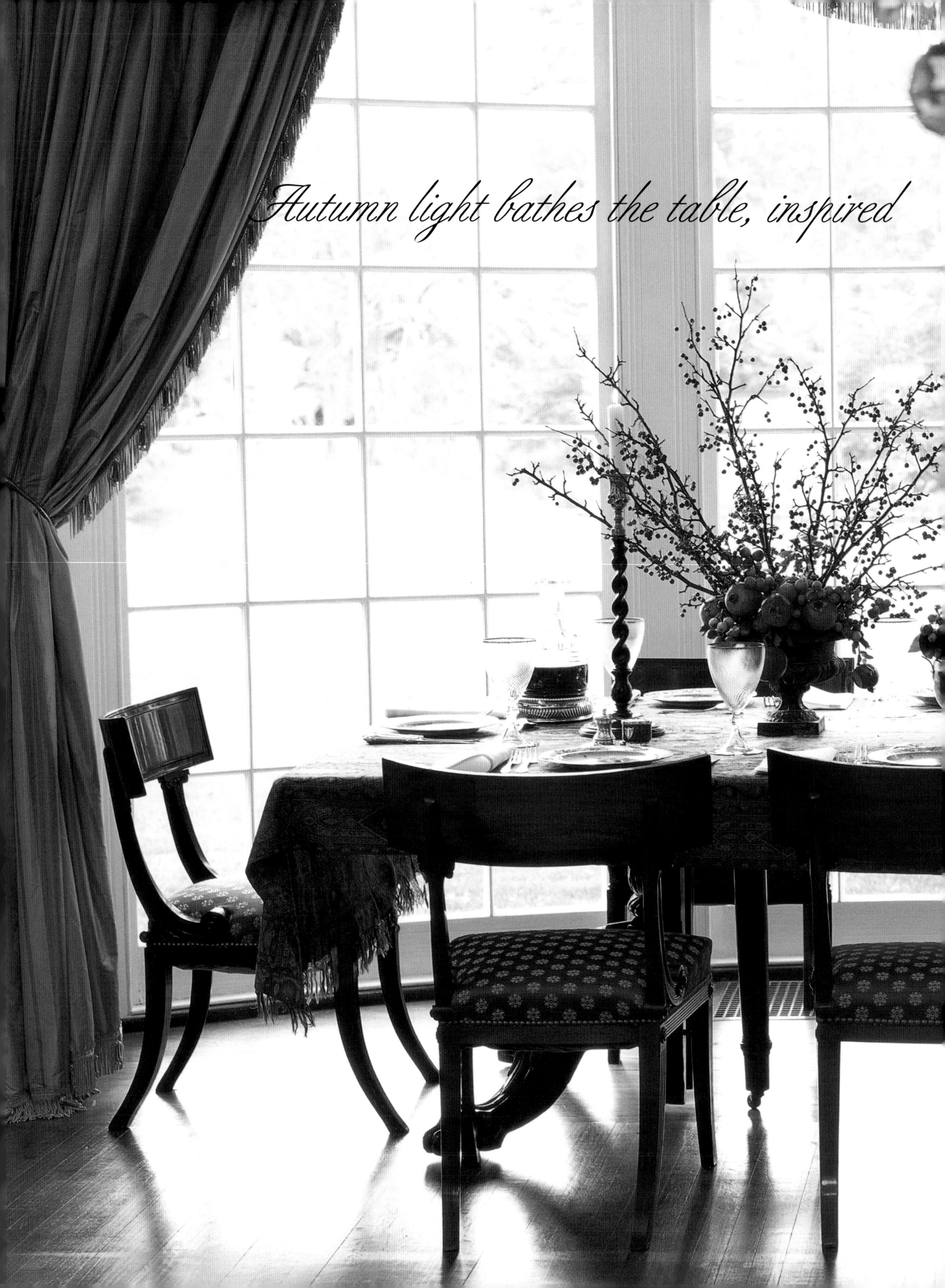

Autumn light bathes the table, inspired

by the colors of a paisley swirl.

The Gazebo Aerie Hides

A Columbus Day Luncheon

Next to the stable, and connected by a wooden bridge, stands a small gazebo of two rooms, one upstairs, one down. The extension was built to be a work nest, a place to settle down to serious business, away from the activity of the main house. The gazebo sits on the highest point on the property, and overlooks miles of rolling Litchfield County fields and hills. The view is so spectacular and so absorbing that it is nearly impossible to get any work done, unless wool-gathering can be considered earnest industry. On this crisp, clear day, I carted my best linen, crystal, china, and silver up to the gazebo for a late formal lunch and a lingering gaze. We stayed long enough to watch the sun descend behind the golden hills.

A handful of crab apples tumble over the rim of the bowl, as if in mid-escape.

DEEP russet florist mums display a brocade richness that is lightened by the jaunty hardy mums with their lime-green eye (opposite). Add sprays of shiny chocolate hypericum berries with lime bracts, and you have an example of how only three elements can create a sumptuous centerpiece. The bouquet owes part of its richness to the range of scale: from small berries, to medium mums, to oversized plump mums. Miniature bouquets at each place setting mirror the larger centerpiece, but with the added element of a few crab apples.

An American Twist on

GUY FAWKES DAY

On November 5, the English celebrate Guy Fawkes Day, an odd festival celebrating Fawkes's failed attempt to blow up Parliament nearly four hundred years ago. On this day, when darkness falls, children and grown-ups all over Britain erect huge bonfires and construct straw effigies of the conspirator, which they toss into the flames. Unlike most holidays that celebrate an actual event, this to me is charming in that it toasts something that didn't happen. So on that same November day, I organized a gathering of friends to celebrate all the happily thwarted events—all the perilous roads not taken— in our lives. As we gathered to warm our hands around the flames, each guest told a poignant story of what could have happened . . . if. It made for an interesting and fascinating evening.

THE local feed store supplied bales of hay, which I stacked and covered with plaid blankets and needlepoint pillows to create outdoor couches. Sharpened green saplings, skewered with sausages, were roasted in the bonfire. Elaborate decorations weren't necessary; a gathering of bittersweet vines (an overzealous weed in these parts) and wooden trugs of apples (opposite) sufficed. The glow from the fire, and various candles lining the table, provided light long into the evening.

A neutral palette of straw, terra-cotta, pale ocher, and woody brown performs best when set off by bold primary colors or patterns, as in the red-and-blue woolen blanket tablecloth.

the Menu

Nancy's Black Bean Chili*

Jalapeño Corn Muffins*

Roasted Knockwurst and Bratwurst

with Assorted Mustards

Spicy Vinaigrette Cabbage Salad

Pear Ginger Pie*

Candied Apples

Warm Mulled Cider

1996 Tapestry Cabernet Sauvignon,

McLauren Vale, Australia

Stacked and scattered bales of straw make fine tables and chairs for buffet dinners.

THE genesis of the party may have been rooted in English history, but the food was strictly international: a big pot of chili, German sausages, and Asian coleslaw (above). The spicy corn muffins (opposite) and chili with a variety of toppings are of Southwestern origin. The chicken-wire basket (opposite) got a makeover with grapevines tied on with raffia, an Italian touch. I chose to serve caramel apples (right) for no other reason than to lessen the load of the orchard glut.

10

For the Man with Everything

A Birthday Celebration

The question is universal: What gift do you give to people who have everything they need? Not everything—no one has everything—but everything they *need*. I struggle with this dilemma constantly, and every year it becomes increasingly difficult to find a meaningful present that isn't just a thoughtless gimmick or a useless luxury. As I get older, I have found that creating an evening filled with laughter, lively conversation, good food, and ample wine shared with dear friends is the most memorable gift you can give someone—an irreplaceable birthday gift that will be remembered far longer than last year's pretty but prosaic cashmere scarf.

Toast your guest of honor with a beautifully decorated table, one of the finest presents you can offer.

WHITE phalaenopsis orchids (left) dance with the candlelight and offer the scene some height and movement. The oversize arrangement (below center) includes a mélange of textured roses, hydrangea, cockscomb, sedum, eucalyptus berries, dried poppy pods, and chocolate cosmos. At each place setting, I set small silver cups of paperwhites, roses, viburnum berries, and chocolate cosmos (below left). I ended the birthday evening on a charming and personal note with individual rum chocolate cakes (opposite) topped with chocolate cosmos and roses.

Create a beautiful story by choosing elements that are complementary in theme but unique in detail.

the Menu

Mushroom, Squash, and Barley Soup

Venison Stroganoff with Egg Noodles

Sautéed Kale

Daire's Fudgy Rum Chocolate Cake*

1998 Hans Lang Spatburgunder

Trocken Joann Maximilian

11

Save Room for Dinner

A Thanksgiving Start

On Thanksgiving Day, all thought goes to the late-day feast. Breakfast and lunch are ignored or rejected in anticipation of the potlatch—turkey, stuffing, mashed potatoes, gravy—to come. For those who gather for their Thanksgiving celebration in the early afternoon, the wait isn't too much of a hardship, but if your tradition dictates that Thanksgiving be held at dinnertime, eight hours without a meal can be too much of a sacrifice. Since I hold Thanksgiving dinner in the early evening, I try to prepare a sustaining-but-not-excessive breakfast for my holiday guests that will keep them nourished until the big event.

THE long wooden table seats all the Thanksgiving guests for an informal breakfast of scrambled eggs, sausage, and waffles. Glass chicken compotes decorate the table in perfect proportion to minipumpkins in the same scale. Although it seems an extravagance for one day of the year, many manufacturers offer turkey-themed plates (these were discovered at a flea market); you can collect all of the same pattern, or you can mix and match single plates.

Blue pressed-glass chicken compotes, holding butter and jams, stand in for the iconic bird.

the Menu

ORANGE PECAN WAFFLES*

WESTERN SCRAMBLED EGGS

BREAKFAST SAUSAGES

TEA AND COFFEE

Red Roses and White at

THE THANKSGIVING FEAST

Traditionally, the color theme for Thanksgiving is quite a dour affair, saturated with deep browns, burgundys, russets, and oranges. But by the time November ends, I feel weighted down by such a heavy palette, and want something breezier before I take on the serious business of Christmas reds and golds. Which is why this Thanksgiving, I chose warm off-whites and whites to carry the day. I moved my dinner table to a sunny enclosed porch just big enough to hold the table and eight chairs. I covered the table in a bleached white matelassé bedspread, and chose a collection of unadorned white porcelain for my serving pieces. On this pristine stage, the food and the company starred.

12

The cut-crystal pattern imitates the delicate quilting on the Portuguese bedspread.

I always try to find an element that plays to or against a dominant texture. See how the English cremeware pitcher (opposite) restrains the more formally detailed tureen (above right). The diamond-etched crystal echoes the diamond quilting on the tablecloth. The rich russet rose 'Estella' (opposite), gathered into a tidy dome, makes a tailored but colorful focal point. Details like these, almost unconscious decisions, are what make the table look so harmonious.

the Menu

David's Squash Soup*

Roasted Capon with Corn Bread Stuffing*

Brussels Sprouts with Pancetta and Cream*

Grandma Beaty's Homemade Noodles*

Susan's Cranberry Relish*

Pear Ginger Pie*

1995 Comte Audoin de Dampierre Champagne Rosé Oeil de Perdrix

Bend tradition: Add dried fruits—cherries, cranberries, or apricots—to the stuffing.

I was feeding relatively few people this Thanksgiving (only eight) when some years I feed thirty. I decided to forgo the usual twenty-pound turkeys; the more succulent capon would be a better choice. The remainder of the meal adhered to tradition, especially the homemade noodles (above), which I have been eating since I was a child in Missouri. The squash soup (opposite) was also a must-have, since the local produce stand was spilling over with a tempting variety of winter squashes.

APPLE CAKE WITH APPLE CIDER GLAZE

A COTTAGE BUFFET *page 175*

8 servings

1 tablespoon vegetable oil

3 cups unsifted all-purpose flour

1 teaspoon salt

1 teaspoon baking powder

1 teaspoon baking soda

1 teaspoon ground cinnamon

2 cups sugar

2 sticks butter, softened

2 large eggs

3 tablespoons milk

2 cups peeled, cored, and chopped Granny Smith or
   MacIntosh apples (about 2 large apples)

1. Preheat oven to 350° F. Grease a Bundt pan with the oil. In a medium bowl, sift together flour, salt, baking powder, baking soda, and cinnamon and set aside.

2. In a large bowl, blend sugar and butter. Add eggs and milk and beat until well combined.

3. Add dry ingredients to sugar mixture and stir until just blended. Fold in apples. Makes a very thick batter.

4. Press batter evenly into prepared pan and bake for 50 to 60 minutes, or until a toothpick inserted into the center comes out clean.

GAME BIRD POT PIE

A LUNCHEON GETAWAY *page 181*

6 servings

3 tablespoons duck fat or olive oil

2½ pounds mixed game bird (pheasant, partridge,
   guinea hen) breasts or chicken breasts, cut into
   2-inch pieces and seasoned with salt and pepper

3 garlic cloves, finely chopped

4 stalks celery, diced

¼ pound carrots, peeled and diced

1 pound pearl onions, peeled and blanched

1 pound sliced mushrooms

5 tablespoons butter

2 tablespoons flour

1 pint heavy cream

2 tablespoons finely chopped fresh rosemary

2 tablespoons finely chopped fresh thyme

½ cup dry sherry

1 teaspoon Worcestershire sauce

½ teaspoon cayenne pepper

1 sheet frozen puff pastry

1 egg at room temperature

2 tablespoons water

1. Preheat oven to 375° F. Season meat with salt and pepper.

2. In a large frying pan, melt 2 tablespoons of duck fat over medium heat. Sauté meat in batches until light brown, about 5 minutes. Set aside.

3. Add remaining fat to pan. Add garlic, celery, carrots, onions, and mushrooms, and cook for 5 minutes. Set aside.

4. Over medium heat, melt butter in a medium saucepan. Stir in flour and cook for 3 minutes. Slowly add heavy cream, whisking the mixture as you add. Bring to a low boil, then reduce heat. Cook until thick, about 5

THE MEAT FOR THE GAME BIRD POT PIE (LEFT) ARRIVED NICELY DRESSED, BUT AFTER NEARLY BREAKING A TOOTH, I RECOMMEND CHECKING THE FLESH FOR BUCKSHOT BEFORE COOKING. SMALL COOKIE CUTTERS OR CANAPÉ CUTTERS CAN BE USED TO EXECUTE THE PASTRY MOTIF (RIGHT).

minutes. Add rosemary, thyme, sherry, Worcestershire sauce, and cayenne.

5. Place meat and vegetables in a 2-quart casserole. Pour cream mixture over meat and vegetables and mix thoroughly.

6. Cut pie pastry 2 inches larger than the top of casserole dish. Place pastry on top of casserole ingredients.

7. Mix egg and water. Brush mixture atop pastry. Bake for 45 minutes or until pastry is puffed and golden. Let the pie rest for 5 minutes before serving.

PECAN TARTS

A LUNCHEON GETAWAY *page 181*

Makes four 4-inch tarts
½ Basic Tart Dough recipe (see page 159)
4 eggs, lightly beaten
1 cup sugar
½ cup light corn syrup

½ cup maple syrup
½ teaspoon vanilla extract
½ cup dark rum
1¾ cups pecan halves

1. Preheat oven to 350° F. Roll out dough and line 4 tart shells. Crimp edges. (Cut out small stars or moons with a cookie cutter, if desired, to decorate tops of tarts.)

2. In a large bowl, combine eggs, sugar, syrups, vanilla, and rum. Mix until well blended. Stir in pecans.

3. Fill shells with mixture, top with dough cut-outs, and place on a baking sheet. Bake for 20 to 25 minutes.

GAME HENS WITH DRIED PLUM STUFFING

SUPPER IN THE COUNTRY *page 187*

4 servings

¾ cup dried plums

½ cup cognac

1 stick butter

½ cup coarsely chopped shallots

1 cup coarsely chopped celery

6 cups cubed stale bread

2 tablespoons plus ¼ teaspoon fresh thyme

2 tablespoons plus ½ teaspoon fresh rosemary

¼ cup chopped parsley

1 teaspoon salt

½ teaspoon freshly ground pepper

2 cups chicken broth

Four 1½- to 2-pound Cornish game hens

4 tablespoons olive oil

1. Preheat oven to 375° F. Soak the plums in cognac for 20 minutes. Drain and reserve cognac.

2. In a large pan, over medium heat, melt butter and add shallots, plums, and celery, and sauté until translucent.

3. Add bread, 2 tablespoons thyme, 2 tablespoons rosemary, the parsley, salt, and pepper, and moisten with chicken broth and reserved cognac.

4. Stuff the birds and coat with olive oil. Sprinkle with remaining thyme and rosemary and roast for 45 minutes to 1 hour.

SHORT RIBS WITH SPICY LEMON CAPER SAUCE

HALLOWEEN SURPRISES *page 198*

6 to 8 servings

4 pounds beef short ribs, cut into 2-inch pieces

Salt and freshly ground pepper

¼ pound salt pork, cubed

3 pounds onions, thinly sliced

2 bay leaves

½ teaspoon ground cloves

2 tablespoons tomato paste

6 to 8 cups cold water

2 slices dark rye bread (stale or toasted)

Juice and zest of 1 lemon

6 tablespoons capers

1 cup chopped parsley

1. Preheat oven to 350° F. Sprinkle short ribs with salt and pepper.

2. In a large flame-proof casserole or Dutch oven, brown salt pork on medium heat until rendered and crisp. (Be careful not to let the pieces burn.) Remove from pan and reserve.

3. To the same casserole, add short ribs in batches and brown on all sides. Remove to a platter.

4. Add onions to the fat and cook, stirring occasionally, until transparent. Add bay leaves, cloves, and tomato paste, and cook for 2 minutes. Add 6 cups of water and bring to a boil.

5. Return short ribs to casserole and bake for 1½ hours or until tender. Add more water if necessary.

6. Remove ribs from casserole. Cover with foil and keep warm. Skim off fat from liquid. Discard bay leaf.

7. Bring liquid back to a boil and reduce for 3 or 4 minutes. Meanwhile, place bread in a food processor or blender and process for bread crumbs. Add bread crumbs to reduced liquid. Add 4 tablespoons lemon juice,

CAPERS, USED IN THE SHORT RIBS SAUCE, ARE BEST WHEN SMALL. THE MOST PRIZED FRENCH CAPERS ARE LABELED NON-PAREIL.

lemon zest, and capers, and reduce for 2 or 3 minutes.

8. Reduce heat. Adjust seasoning and add more lemon juice if necessary. Pour sauce over meat and garnish with reserved salt pork and parsley. Serve immediately.

APPLE PEAR CRISP

HALLOWEEN SURPRISES *page 198*

6 to 8 servings

2 tablespoons butter at room temperature,
  plus 6 tablespoons melted
5 Granny Smith or MacIntosh apples, peeled,
  cored, and sliced
5 Bartlett pears, peeled, cored, and sliced

Juice and zest of 1 lemon
1 cup steel-cut oats
¾ cup flour
1 cup light brown sugar
1 teaspoon cinnamon
½ teaspoon ground cardamom

1. Preheat oven to 375° F. Grease a 13 x 9-inch glass pan with 2 tablespoons butter. Toss the apples and pears in the pan with the lemon juice and zest and arrange in the pan.

2. In a medium bowl, mix the oats, flour, sugar, and spices. Add melted butter and mix well. Evenly sprinkle oat mixture over fruit. Bake for 40 minutes.

NANCY'S BLACK BEAN CHILI

GUY FAWKES DAY *page 216*

6 to 8 servings

4 tablespoons olive oil

8 garlic cloves, sliced

1 large onion, coarsely chopped

1 each red, yellow, and jalapeño pepper, coarsely
  chopped

1½ pounds ground sirloin

2 tablespoons chili powder

1 pound black beans, cooked

One 28-ounce can crushed tomatoes, with juice

½ cup water

Salt and freshly ground pepper to taste

For garnish: 1 bunch scallions, diced, ¼ pound
  Cheddar cheese, shredded, and 2 cups sour cream

1. In a large saucepan, heat olive oil over medium-high heat. Sauté garlic, onion, and peppers for 5 minutes.

2. Add ground sirloin and chili powder and sauté until meat browns, about 5 minutes.

3. Add black beans, tomatoes, and water, and bring to a boil. Reduce heat and simmer for 30 minutes.

4. Serve chili with garnishes in individual bowls.

JALAPEÑO CORN MUFFINS

GUY FAWKES DAY *page 216*

Makes 12

1 teaspoon plus ¼ cup canola oil

1½ cups all-purpose flour

¼ cup stone-ground cornmeal

¼ cup sugar

2 teaspoons baking powder

½ teaspoon salt

1 cup milk at room temperature

2 large eggs, slightly beaten

1 fresh jalapeño pepper, seeded and finely minced

1 cup corn kernels

¾ cup grated Cheddar cheese

1. Preheat oven to 400° F. Grease muffin tin with 1 teaspoon oil and set aside.

2. In a large mixing bowl, whisk together flour, cornmeal, sugar, baking powder, and salt. Add milk, eggs, jalapeño, and remaining ¼ cup oil. Stir until just blended.

3. Fold in corn and cheese. Divide batter evenly among muffin cups. They should not be more than two-thirds full.

4. Bake for 20 to 25 minutes until golden.

Black bean chili toppings and condiments served in earthen ramekins rest on a basket tray (left). Peppery crystallized ginger makes a fine foil for the sweet pears in the dessert (right).

PEAR GINGER PIE

GUY FAWKES DAY *page 216*

Makes one 9-inch pie
1 Basic Tart Dough recipe (see page 159)
6 to 8 Anjou pears, peeled and sliced
¼ cup minced crystallized ginger

¼ cup sugar
Juice and grated zest of ½ lemon
2 tablespoons flour

1. Preheat oven to 400° F. Roll out half the dough and place in the bottom of a 9-inch pie plate.
2. In a large bowl, mix the pears, ginger, sugar, and lemon juice and zest. Sprinkle with flour and toss fruit well.
3. Roll out remaining dough and place on top of pie; crimp the edges. Bake for 45 minutes to 1 hour or until golden.

Daire's Fudgy Rum Chocolate Cake   A Birthday Celebration   *page 223*
This recipe first appears in Happy Birthday. See the Summer section for the recipe on page 157.

ORANGE PECAN WAFFLES

A THANKSGIVING START   *page 227*

8 servings

4 eggs, separated

1 cup buttermilk

1 cup orange juice

1 stick butter, melted

1 teaspoon vanilla extract

1½ cups sour cream

¼ cup sugar

2¾ cups all-purpose flour

1½ teaspoons baking powder

1½ teaspoons baking soda

1 cup pecans, finely chopped

2 tablespoons grated orange zest

Maple syrup for serving

1. Preheat waffle iron. In a large bowl combine egg yolks, buttermilk, orange juice, melted butter, vanilla, sour cream, and sugar. Beat well.

2. In another bowl, combine flour, baking powder, baking soda, pecans, and zest. Stir into liquid mixture, being careful not to overmix.

3. Beat egg whites until stiff and fold into batter.

4. Spray waffle iron with nonstick cooking spray, and cook waffles according to manufacturer's directions.

5. Serve immediately with hot maple syrup.

DAVID'S SQUASH SOUP

THE THANKSGIVING FEAST   *page 232*

8 servings

4½ cups cooked and puréed butternut squash

1½ cans (13¾ ounces) chicken broth

1½ tablespoons salt

½ tablespoon pepper

½ teaspoon cayenne pepper

1 tablespoon curry powder

½ bottle Tio Pepe Gonzalez Byass Jerez dry sherry

3 tablespoons butter

½ cup sour cream

½ cup heavy cream

1. In a large soup pot, combine the squash purée, chicken broth, salt, pepper, cayenne, and curry powder. Bring to a boil. Reduce heat and simmer uncovered approximately 1 hour to reduce soup by one-third.

2. Add sherry and simmer another 30 minutes. Remove from heat and swirl in butter, sour cream, and heavy cream. Serve immediately.

ROASTED CAPON WITH CORN BREAD STUFFING

THE THANKSGIVING FEAST *page 232*

4 to 6 servings

1 pound breakfast sausage, cut in ½-inch pieces

1 large onion, chopped into medium dice

2 apples, peeled, cored, and coarsely chopped

1 pound of corn bread, cut into 1-inch cubes

2 sticks butter, melted

2 teaspoons thyme

2 teaspoons sage

Salt and freshly ground pepper to taste

One 18.5-ounce can chicken broth

One 6- to 7-pound capon

2 tablespoons olive oil

1. Preheat oven to 450° F. In a large skillet over medium heat, brown the sausage. Add onion and sauté until translucent. Add apples and cook 1 minute.

2. Add corn bread, butter, thyme, sage, and salt and pepper to taste, and cook for 5 minutes, mixing thoroughly.

3. Slowly add the chicken broth until bread is moistened.

4. Wash capon thoroughly and dry with paper towels. Stuff the cavity of the capon. Place in a roasting pan, rub with olive oil, and sprinkle very liberally with salt and pepper.

5. Place bird in oven and roast for 30 minutes. Reduce heat to 375° F and roast for 1 hour 15 minutes, basting three times.

THE TENDERNESS OF CAPON (LEFT), A NEUTERED YOUNG MALE CHICKEN, IS DUE TO THE ACCUMULATION OF FAT STORED IN THE MUSCLES. THE BRUSSELS SPROUTS ARE TRANSFORMED WITH THE ADDITION OF PANCETTA AND CREAM (RIGHT).

BRUSSELS SPROUTS WITH PANCETTA AND CREAM

THE THANKSGIVING FEAST *page 232*

6 servings
2 pounds fresh Brussels sprouts
¼ pound pancetta, diced

½ cup heavy cream
Salt and freshly ground pepper

1. Blanch Brussels sprouts until just cooked, about 8 minutes.
2. In a sauté pan cook pancetta over medium heat until crisp. Drain and discard fat, if necessary, leaving 2 table-spoons in the pan along with the pancetta.
3. Add cream to the pan and reduce by one-third. Add Brussels sprouts and gently heat through. Season with salt and pepper to taste. Serve immediately.

GRANDMA BEATY'S HOMEMADE NOODLES

THE THANKSGIVING FEAST *page 232*

6 to 8 servings
3 large eggs
2 tablespoons heavy cream
1 tablespoon vegetable oil
¼ teaspoon salt

¼ teaspoon baking powder
¾ teaspoon curry powder
2½ to 3 cups all-purpose flour
6 cups chicken broth
One 15-ounce can cream of chicken soup

1. Preheat oven to 350° F. In a large bowl, beat together the eggs, cream, oil, salt, baking powder, and curry powder.
2. On a large surface, mound 2 cups of flour and make a well in the middle. Add egg mixture. With a fork, incorporate flour into egg, adding more flour if necessary to make a stiff dough.
3. Roll out dough to ⅛-inch thickness. Sprinkle with flour and roll up tightly like a jelly roll. Make ⅛-inch-wide slices. Unroll noodle strips and let dry for 15 minutes.
4. Bring broth to a boil in a Dutch oven. Add the cream of chicken soup. Add noodles to broth and stir well. Bring back to a boil, then at once remove from heat, put into oven, and bake for 30 minutes. Serve immediately.

THE TRICK TO GIVING THE CRANBERRY RELISH (LEFT) THE RIGHT TEXTURE IS TO SEND THE INGREDIENTS THROUGH AN OLD-FASHIONED MEAT GRINDER. HOMEMADE NOODLES IN A CREAMY BROTH ARE LADLED FROM A SOUP TUREEN (RIGHT).

SUSAN'S CRANBERRY RELISH

THE THANKSGIVING FEAST *page 232*

Makes 2 cups
One 12-ounce bag fresh cranberries

1 navel orange
¾ cup sugar

1. Rinse cranberries and cut orange into eighths. Pass cranberries and orange through an old-fashioned meat grinder on the finest blade, or process in batches in a food processor with a steel blade.
2. Add sugar to cranberry-orange mixture and stir well.
3. Refrigerate for 24 hours before serving.

Pear Ginger Pie The Thanksgiving Feast *page 232*
This recipe first appears in Guy Fawkes Day. See page 239 for the recipe.

WINTER

Winter brings unkind
behind doors, attend
Demeter, goddess of
Activity now centers
cozy fireplace. Season
reveries of the garden
fancy and imagination
books become friends
of everything beckons
instincts threaten goo

weather. We huddle
ng to neglected tasks.
ne hearth, rules.
n kitchen stove and
al downtime permits
to come. Flights of
flower. Neglected
again. Reorganization
but hibernation
d intentions.

1. A JOYEUX NOËL   2. AN INFORMAL TEA   3. THE CHRISTMAS PARTY

7. A BIRTHDAY DINNER   8. A MINIMALIST LUNCH   9. AN IMPROMPTU LUNCH

Winter in Paris for
A JOYEUX NOËL

In the winter, Paris lures me with its charms. Walking among the gray skies and matching gray buildings of this city feels to me like a shadowy prowl through an old black-and-white photograph. If the muted colors turn my mood serious, a quick stroll through the flower market liberates it. Startling hues from every part of the spectrum and blooms from every corner of the globe are available for a few francs. It is not difficult to find inspiration here for a holiday theme. A clutch of dainty rose-red carnations (dianthus) catches my eye and reminds me of a red damask fabric remnant that will serve well as a tablecloth. Green spiral blown-glass stemware I had bought in Italy finds a place at the table, and the rose-red and green Christmas theme is complete.

THE wee carnations inspire a switch from the usual deep Christmas red to more rosy tones for table and presents (below). The mirror (opposite) is surrounded with a garland made from yellow-margined holly with yellow berries, studded with velvety dusty rose and magenta cockscomb.

A single miniature dianthus becomes the catalyst for a whole palette of rosy reds.

Dianthus 'Laced Monarch'

Dianthus caryophyllus Grenadin hybrid, pink

Ranunculus asiaticus orange

Rose 'Peppermint Twist'

Ranunculus asiaticus 'Bloomingdale Hybrid,' rose

Ranunculus asiaticus, magenta

Florist hybrid tea rose, pink

Ranunculus asiaticus 'Bloomingdale Hybrid,' tangerine

Dianthus plumarius

Dianthus modern pink, magenta

The floral elements of the holly garland and carnation centerpiece combine forces in a pedestal vase.

2

Celebrating Christmas with

AN INFORMAL TEA

The holiday season can be a stressful time, when our limited social allowances become stretched to the maximum. Dinners, cocktail parties, and family gatherings so fill up our entertaining schedule that there is scant time left to accommodate all our friends or obligations. I have found that one way to catch up with friends, without burdening them with a formal commitment, is to invite them to stop by for a cup of tea. I have a cozy room at the stable that I decorate with greens and pinecones, nothing elaborate, collected from the property. I make small tea sandwiches and a pound cake (also wonderful grilled with butter for breakfast). Once we finish our tea and sandwiches, I invariably offer my visitor a small gift.

Fairy lights, a basket of pinecones, and well-wrapped gifts adorn a merry Christmas tea.

the Menu

Rosa's Cucumber, Watercress,
and Chicken Salad Tea Sandwiches

Otha's Pound Cake*

Coffee and Assorted Teas

Tinsel and Glitter Highlight

THE CHRISTMAS PARTY

For the last few years I have given my largest holiday party at Weatherpebble, the cottage I have been living in while Weatherstone, which burned to the ground, is being rebuilt. Weatherpebble is a very small house, but it does have one large room that originally housed carriages. The room is paneled in dark-stained pine, which absorbs much of the natural light. For this reason, I decided that silver, which reflects and disperses light so effectively, would be the dominant color of my holiday party. I had found an airy dried weed that looked almost like baby's breath, sprayed it silver, then added silver glitter. A large arrangement of the silver weed, buttressed by two smaller gatherings, made an effective but simple centerpiece. To reiterate the glittering theme, I hung silver foil tinsel from wreaths and garlands, and draped pounds more on the thirteen-foot Christmas tree.

I gathered all the silver I could find, some inexpensive plate—the beakers (below) cost $14—and some prized sterling, to set the table. I wove silver-sprayed ivy poked with small sprays of the silver weed through the candelabra arms, and dusted it all with glitter. Each place setting was marked with a small silver foil box filled with marzipan fruit (below right), tied with silver thread, and topped with—again—a spray of the silver weed. Proof positive that all that glitters is not gold.

Lustrous, shiny silver bounces pieces of magical light across the room.

A lifelong collection of glass ornaments hides beneath a curtain of tinsel.

AFTER years of creating chic Christmas trees, I decided it was time to go back to my childhood tree and load on the tinsel. It certainly helped convey my silver theme. Dressing the thirteen-foot pine, cut from a nearby tree farm, was an all-day production made more difficult by the dogs, who made a game of removing tinsel and ornaments from the bottom branches. I took a tamer approach for the fireplace, which was draped with a garland of evergreens. I crowned the ceiling lamps with a simple wreath hung with satin ribbons.

An Intimate Old-Fashioned

CHRISTMAS EVE GATHERING

Some years Christmas Eve is a quiet affair, and I can forgo a large formal dinner for an intimate gathering in the gazebo overlooking snow-covered hills. The small snug room calls for a relaxed theme: basket nests of juniper and lady apples, homemade cookie ornaments, and wooden candlesticks tied with a spray of greens. So that the table wouldn't look too rustic, I added one fancy element that would elevate the festivities: a green-and-white plaid silk taffeta tablecloth (an end-of-bolt remnant) to match the candle ribbons. Glass service plates and soup bowls, recycled from a Fourth of July picnic, were garnished with a pinecone candle and a snip of juniper, which, fortunately, I remembered to remove stealthily before the soup was poured.

the Menu

CREAM OF CHESTNUT SOUP

CONTRE FILET IN PÉRIGOURDINE SAUCE

WILD RICE

PUREE OF BROCCOLI

POPOVERS

BÛCHE DE NOËL

CAROLYNE'S FAVORITE SUGAR COOKIES*

1997 CHÂTEAU HAUT-MILON PAUILLAC,
    BORDEAUX

A COLLECTION OF GLASS SANTA ORNAMENTS (ABOVE LEFT) AND HOMEMADE COOKIES ICED IN RED AND
WHITE (ABOVE RIGHT) LEND AN OLD-FASHIONED AIR TO THE CHRISTMAS TREE (RIGHT).

Green and White Palette at
A New Year's Dinner

By the time December ends, I am bored with the constant coupling of red and green. I am also becoming antsy for spring, in part thanks to the onslaught of gardening catalogues that start pouring in. The dark winter skies and dirty snow-slushed streets make me long for the new green of spring. But I have three months to go before any of these hopes can be realized, which is why I opted for a slate of greens for this winter dinner. Boxwood clippings pushed into floral foam held in porcelain baskets serve as faux topiaries, their rigid form adding structured formality. They flank a bowl of green grapes punctuated with dark-green lemon leaves. More sprigs of boxwood, magnolia, and eucalyptus berries and leaves form a garland and matching wreath. Bright color may be absent for now, but texture fills the void.

GREEN—from pale pistachio and lemon-lime to mossy silver grays—cools the atmosphere when set against a white background. Shiny foil wrappings (top right) echo the same array of greens as in the topiaries (below left and right) and mantelpiece decorations.

Texture hard at work: Cut crystal, ornamental gold, and embroidered organdy share the same tailored crispness as the gathering of greens.

the ᴍenu

WILD MUSHROOM SOUP WITH SOUR MASH

PORK LOIN WITH KUMQUATS*

STUFFED ARTICHOKE HEARTS

FRISÉE SALAD WITH STILTON AND GRAPES

GRAND MARNIER SOUFFLÉ

1997 BACHELET-RAMONET

CHASSAGNE-MONTRACHET PREMIER CRU

6

Retreat to the Greenhouse for
A Winter Luncheon

During the winter, while my back is turned on the garden, I take refuge in the greenhouse. Joanne, the gardener at Weatherstone, makes use of the dormant season to turn this twenty-five-foot square into an oasis of fertility. Citrus trees, forced bulbs, azalea standards, bay topiaries, miniature roses, cascading ivies, and tropical orchids are packed from floor to rafter. As soon as I push open the glasshouse door, the warm air, permeated with the seductive scent of orange blossoms, makes me feel as if I have arrived at a tiny island retreat, a welcome contrast to the sterility of the frozen ground outside. Lunch in the greenhouse usually lasts well into the afternoon. I hesitate to return to the reality of January.

The Zodiac Determines

A BIRTHDAY DINNER

Aquarians are said to be idealistic and inventive; Capricorns are worrywarts, but steadfast friends. Accommodating these two forces for a birthday celebration proved challenging—not because these earth and air signs are incompatible, but because I had already exhausted every original decorating idea and recipe during the holiday season. Therefore, I looked to the flower market to turn my head away from overused heavy reds to discover something new and fresh. Whenever I run out of steam, the shelves and floors packed with imported flowers never fail to inspire me. Spying an irresistible soft yellow double tulip, and using the tones of that flower as a starting point, I created the Capricorn-Aquarian birthday table.

Gold vermeil candlesticks and flatware formalize the gaiety of the centerpiece.

ROSES, hellebores, tulips, viburnum, mums, anemones, alliums, hyacinth, ivy, and eucalyptus berries, held in a *porcelaine de Paris* pedestal vase (opposite), are flanked by two smaller reproduction porcelain baskets (above) filled with limes, hellebores, ivy, grapes, and eucalyptus berries, which reflect the tones of yellow and green in the centerpiece bouquet. The silver artichokes (right) foretell an ingredient in the swordfish entrée.

CORN SOUP WITH RED PEPPER PURÉE*

GRILLED SWORDFISH WITH ARTICHOKES,
TOMATOES, AND OLIVES*

PURÉED CELERIAC

ENDIVE, WALNUTS, AND ROQUEFORT SALAD

TAPIOCA SOUFFLÉ

LOUIS ROEDERER BRUT PREMIER, CHAMPAGNE

1998 DEISS RIESLING ENGELGARTEN, ALSACE

the Menu

The contrast of sharp Niçoise olives and soft,
mellow fresh artichoke hearts graces the grilled fish.

ADD A SUMMERY NOTE TO A WINTER BIRTHDAY CELEBRATION WITH FRESH SWORDFISH STEAK GARNISHED
WITH RIPE TOMATOES, OLIVES, AND ARTICHOKES (ABOVE).

$$8$$

The Blizzard Influences

A MINIMALIST LUNCH

A friend accuses me of being steeped in eighteenth- and nineteenth-century decoration; he says I could never be a modernist or a minimalist. To prove him wrong, to show him that I could "do" pared down, I invited him to lunch, which happened to occur on the day of a mean blizzard. The white-out weather influenced the table's theme: icy white and no doodads. An earlier trip to the housewares outlet produced a clean collection of inexpensive basic china plates and soup bowls. I also bought two simple juice glasses to use as salt and pepper cellars, and picked up some stout stemware. The look, I thought, was very modern, but I couldn't help myself. I needed a touch of razzmatazz: a cluster of wicked red gerber daisies and cactus dahlias in stout white pitchers.

Tails of Ivy Rescue

AN IMPROMPTU LUNCH

Friends arrived in town unexpectedly, calling to say they were in the area, and could they drop by for lunch? I had just returned from a trip the night before so was not prepared to festoon the table with cut flowers. The greenhouse was in a slump; the forced bulbs had come and gone, but Joanne had started some slips of ivy to root. Perfect. Especially since I have Wedgwood plates with an ivy-decorated rim. I grabbed two rusty urns from the horde of pots and transplanted the ivy tails, snipping a few to wrap around the rolled napkins. A few more strands of ivy were tucked around the iron lattice hurricane lamp (held in place with a dab of florist clay). The green glass stemware was the last to go in place, then all was ready for the impulsive visitors.

Real ivy tails and ivy-painted plates form an alluring alliance.

WHEN most people think centerpiece, they think flowers, but this doesn't always have to be the case. Ivy,

bare branches, found objects—whatever catches your eye can be enlisted to substitute. A friend told me that while cleaning

his backyard of wild growth, he came across an eager grapevine. While struggling to pull down the vine, he thought: I should

do something with this interesting thing with peeling bark. So he scrunched and spiraled the vine into a long garland and

centered it on his weathered garden dining table. The effect was charming evidence that it pays to think outside convention.

the Menu

Sweet Potato and Pear Soup*

Gougonettes of Sole aux Poivre Vert

Green Salad

Crème Caramel

1997 Gros Bourgogne Haute Côtes de Nuits Blanc

Nodding to Cupid

A Ladies' Luncheon

The hearts-and-flowers frills of Valentine's Day delight my women friends, but the charm of the holiday seems lost on their significant others. The men might put up with the notion that flowers or perfume or chocolates are in order, but these offerings require only a quick phone call and a credit card. Since I, like my girlfriends, am enchanted by a day devoted to romance, I invite them (unattached, of course) for a lunch decorated with all the lacy bits that would be lost on their husbands. At each place setting, I pose a carnation and rose heart constructed on a base of floral foam that they can take home to their own Valentines. It's a gentle nudge to let the men know how much they are missing.

Lonely Hearts Band at

A VALENTINE'S DAY DINNER

On another Valentine's Day, I decided to include the men, but I knew that I needed to tone down the romantic theme. A drum table with shelves of Moroccan leather-bound books set a more masculine tone when moved beside the weathered center-hall door. The atmospheric background now settled, I decide pastel pinks had best be omitted; neutral white flowers seemed safer. Crimson glassware, sterling silver flatware and service plates, crisp linens, and black candles suited the setting. But I refused to hide my feminine side: Arching, whimsical branches of forced prunus added a dainty touch. As long as I remembered to chill a few extra bottles of champagne, I was sure the men wouldn't mind.

offered a gift (below) at each place setting, containing a personal token of affection keyed to the recipient's passionate interests. Instead of a centerpiece, I placed small silver beakers at each plate filled with white roses, ranunculus, and anemones, and sent the beakers home with the guests as party favors. One lucky guest received a heart-shaped floral foam form studded with 'Black Magic' roses (opposite) nestled in tissue paper and boxed.

"Hearts are not had as a gift but hearts are earned." – YEATS

Evoking Warm Memories at

A SIMPLE SOUP DINNER

Soup sustains me. It is a comforting, warm, soothing friend greeting me at the kitchen door. The smell of soup simmering on the stove conjures up memories of childhood, when Mom's chicken noodle soup could cure any ailment, physical or mental. Soup draws people together, warming hearts as well as stomachs. In northwestern Connecticut, when the snow covers every inch of the ground and has forced our doors shut, Nancy, the Weatherstone cook, gathers her ingredients in one pot, and the aroma soon drifts throughout the house, erasing our winter blues. A table adorned with hot bowls of soup and a few bulb vases of scented hyacinth allows us to enjoy the comforts of being housebound during a storm.

It takes few ingredients to make a welcoming soup: vegetables form the stock, while shrimp and beans give it body.

Sharing a pot of soup among friends warms even the most frigid of winter's nights.

the Menu

SHRIMP AND WHITE BEAN SOUP*

SALAD WITH BRIE EN CROUTE

POACHED PEARS IN PORT WINE

1999 LOUIS JADOT POUILLY-FUISSÉ

OTHA'S POUND CAKE

AN INFORMAL TEA   *page 259*

8 servings

1 cup milk

2 sticks unsalted butter

4 eggs

3 cups sugar

3 cups all-purpose flour

1 teaspoon baking powder

1 teaspoon salt

1. Preheat oven to 300° F. In a medium saucepan, heat milk and butter to boiling, then let cool.

2. Beat eggs with an electric mixer. Continue beating while gradually adding sugar.

3. Add milk-and-butter mixture to eggs and mix well. Sift flour, baking powder, and salt together. Add to mixture and beat very hard with an electric mixer (about 5 minutes).

4. Grease an angel food cake pan. Pour batter into pan. Bake for 90 minutes, or until a tester comes out clean. Cut recipe in half for an 8½ x 4½-inch loaf pan.

CAROLYNE'S FAVORITE SUGAR COOKIES

CHRISTMAS EVE GATHERING   *page 270*

Yield depends on size of cookie cutters

3 cups flour

3 sticks butter

1½ cups light brown sugar

1 teaspoon salt

3 teaspoons cinnamon

1 teaspoon ground cloves

1 teaspoon ground nutmeg

3 to 4 tablespoons milk

1. Preheat oven to 350° F. Place all ingredients except milk in the bowl of a food processor. Pulse 10 times. Add 2 tablespoons of milk and process, adding milk as necessary until dough forms a ball.

2. Refrigerate the dough for 1 hour. Roll out dough to ¼-inch thickness and cut out with cookie cutters.

3. Place cookies on a greased baking sheet and bake until brown, about 8 minutes.

PORK LOIN WITH KUMQUATS

A NEW YEAR'S DINNER *page 277*

8 servings

One 4- to 5-pound boneless pork loin

½ cup Louisiana hot sauce

2 cups chicken broth

2 pints kumquats

2 pints cherry tomatoes

3 tablespoons olive oil

1 teaspoon salt

½ cup orange marmalade

1. Preheat oven to 375° F. Place the pork loin in a large roasting pan. Pour hot sauce over pork. Add chicken broth to pan. Cover pork and cook for 30 minutes.

2. Add kumquats to the pan and re-cover. Coat tomatoes with olive oil and salt and place on baking sheet.

3. Return both pans to the oven and roast for another 30 minutes.

4. Remove pans and preheat broiler. Set aside tomatoes. Coat the roast pork with orange marmalade. Broil until light brown and bubbling, about 5 minutes.

5. Slice the pork and slightly fan the slices on a platter garnished with the kumquats and the tomatoes. Spoon about ½ cup of sauce over the roast and serve.

CORN SOUP WITH RED PEPPER PURÉE

A BIRTHDAY DINNER *page 284*

6 servings

4 tablespoons butter

2 cups chopped shallots

6 cups fresh or frozen corn kernels

4 cups chicken broth

1 bay leaf

¼ cup plus 3 tablespoons heavy cream

½ cup milk

1 tablespoon salt

1 teaspoon white pepper

1 teaspoon chili powder

2 large red peppers, roasted, skinned, and seeded

1 teaspoon white vinegar

1. In a medium soup pot over medium heat, melt butter. Add shallots and sauté until translucent. Add corn, chicken broth, and bay leaf. Bring to a boil. Reduce heat and simmer for 10 minutes.

2. Cool soup, puree in a food processor or blender, and put through a fine sieve.

3. Return soup to pot and add ¼ cup heavy cream, milk, salt, pepper, and chili powder. Return to medium heat and cook for 5 more minutes.

4. Put roasted peppers in the bowl of a food processor or blender. Add 3 tablespoons heavy cream, salt and pepper to taste, and vinegar. Blend until smooth.

5. Pour soup into bowls and drizzle pepper puree. Serve immediately.

GRILLED SWORDFISH WITH ARTICHOKES, TOMATOES, AND OLIVES

A BIRTHDAY DINNER *page 284*

4 servings

¼ cup plus 3 tablespoons olive oil

1 medium onion, diced

5 garlic cloves, diced

One 14-ounce can artichoke hearts

4 medium tomatoes, peeled, seeded, and diced

30 small black olives

½ cup chopped basil

½ cup chopped parsley

Salt and freshly ground pepper to taste

Juice of 1 lemon

1 teaspoon salt

2 teaspoons pepper

2 pounds swordfish steaks, ½ inch thick

1. In a medium saucepan over medium-high heat, add ¼ cup olive oil, onion, and garlic and sauté until translucent, 4 or 5 minutes.

2. Cut artichoke hearts in quarters, add to pan, and sauté 3 or 4 minutes. Add tomatoes and olives and cook 10 minutes.

3. Add basil, parsley, salt, and pepper and cook 2 more minutes. Set aside.

4. Combine 3 tablespoons olive oil, lemon juice, salt, and pepper. Marinate steaks for 10 minutes.

5. Sear steaks on a grill or grill pan for approximately 5 minutes per side.

6. Place on a warm platter and serve with artichoke-tomato sauté.

IT IS BEST TO USE FRESH ARTICHOKES (LEFT) FOR THE SWORDFISH, BUT CANNED OR FROZEN HEARTS MAY BE SUBSTITUTED. THE FLAVOR OF THE SWEET POTATO AND PEAR SOUP IS ENHANCED BY THE ADDITION OF PEAR BRANDY (RIGHT).

SWEET POTATO AND PEAR SOUP

AN IMPROMPTU LUNCH *page 291*

6 servings

3 large sweet potatoes, peeled and cubed

2 medium russet potatoes, peeled and cubed

4 cups chicken broth

¾ cup chopped shallots

2-inch piece of ginger, peeled and minced

4 tablespoons butter

½ cup orange juice

Salt and freshly ground pepper to taste

2 Bartlett pears, peeled and coarsely chopped

¼ cup pear brandy

Zest of 1 lime

1. Simmer potatoes in chicken broth until potatoes are cooked through. Meanwhile, over low heat, sauté shallots and ginger in 2 tablespoons butter for about 5 minutes.

2. Drain the potatoes, reserving liquid. Puree potatoes, shallots, ginger, orange juice, and reserved liquid with an immersion blender or in a food processor in batches. Process until smooth. Return soup to pan and season with salt and pepper. (Add more chicken stock for a thinner soup.)

3. Over medium heat, sauté pears in the remaining 2 tablespoons butter for 5 minutes. Remove the pears from the stove and add the pear brandy. Return the pears to the stove and flambé pears until the alcohol burns off. Add pears and pan juices to the soup. Reheat soup.

4. Pour into individual bowls and top with lime zest.

SHRIMP AND WHITE BEAN SOUP

A SIMPLE SOUP DINNER *page 301*

6 to 8 servings

1 red onion, chopped

3 shallots, minced

8 garlic cloves, peeled and sliced

2 cups finely chopped celery

2 medium carrots, peeled and finely chopped

¼ cup olive oil

1-pound bag of dried cannellini beans or cranberry
 beans, cooked according to package directions

One 28-ounce can plum tomatoes, chopped, with juice

2 tablespoons fresh rosemary, finely chopped

2 tablespoons fresh thyme, finely chopped

1 teaspoon dried oregano

2 bay leaves

Salt and pepper to taste

6 to 8 cups fish or clam broth

2 pounds large shrimp, shelled and deveined

Juice and zest of 1 lemon

½ cup finely chopped fresh parsley

½ teaspoon red pepper flakes

1. In a large soup pot over medium heat, sauté onion, shallots, garlic, celery, and carrots in olive oil until translucent.

2. Add cooked beans, tomatoes, rosemary, thyme, oregano, bay leaves, salt, and pepper. Simmer for 5 minutes, stirring occasionally.

3. Add fish or clam broth. Simmer for 45 to 60 minutes, until soup thickens.

4. Add shrimp, lemon juice and zest, parsley, and pepper flakes. Cook until shrimp are just pink and firm, about 3 minutes. Serve immediately.

If you think of a dinner party as the telling of a good story, the elements of the table–plates, flatware, stemware, linens, centerpiece–would be the setting. The food would be the plot. As you tell the story, you pace the action (the courses of the meal), and you create an atmosphere (the theme of the table). But there is one factor that sets a gripping story apart from a dull one: the details. On the following pages, the story unfolds.

DETAILS

Fashion in table setting is not a modern phenomenon. We have been dressing our tables ever since we've actually had tables. No matter how informally, or formally, our meals are expressed, it comforts me to know that the ritual of setting the table has deep roots in the past. So the next time your teenager rolls his eyes and asks why he needs to use a napkin, you will be able to state with authority: "To protect your costly ruff, my dear."

NAPKINS

In Roman times, diners traveled with their own cloths. One oversized cloth was tied around the neck and used to wipe fingers (except for knives, personal eating utensils were unknown); another was used to wrap leftover food to take home. Through much of the Middle Ages, tablecloths were used as napkins, but by the late Middle Ages, huge decorative napkins with fringe had appeared. In Europe in the sixteenth century, napkins were starched and folded into intricate forms representing animals, boats, flowers, and birds. The fashion of fussy napkin folding lasted until the nineteenth century, when it was considered vulgar, as it is by some to this day. By the late seventeenth century, smaller delicate cloths were tucked into the collars of the wealthy to protect their expensive lace ruffs. In the early nineteenth century, the cloths had migrated to laps, where they have remained. Now, of course, the napkin has become a gesture more than a tool. We are not actually supposed to dirty our pristine white napkin, but use it to dab delicately at our lips.

THE TABLECLOTH

Our early domestic lives were carried out without much privacy. We did not have specialized rooms for specialized activities. Cooking, sleeping, and entertaining were usually performed in one central room. Our furniture was rough and handmade. Well-to-do Romans would cover the unsightliness of the wood with a cloth, which had a dual purpose. Since napkins were little used in Western society until the sixteenth century, tablecloths were used to clean hands and face. The best of the cloths were woven in Damascus, Syria, and to this day, damask is still a much-desired table covering. In late medieval times, diners ate on one side of the table

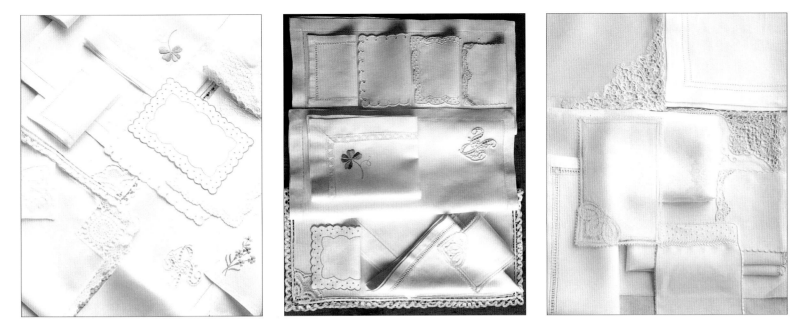

FORMAL LINENS MAY BE EMBROIDERED, INITIALED, EDGED IN LACE OR TATTING, OR PULLWORK. NAPKINS OF

PRINTED FABRIC, OR WITH BOLDER EMBROIDERY, AND FRINGE WORK ARE MORE SUITABLE FOR INFORMAL SETTINGS.

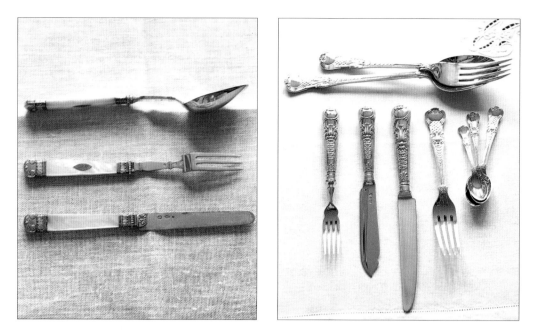

FLATWARE HANDLES CAN BE MADE FROM MOTHER-OF-PEARL, VERMEIL, SILVER, PLATE, PLASTIC,

BAMBOO, BONE, OR WOOD. NO MATTER WHAT THE MATERIAL, SPOTS ON KNIVES, FORKS, AND

SPOONS SHOULD BE REMOVED WITH A SOFT POLISHING CLOTH ONCE THE TABLE IS SET.

facing entertainment or pensioners in the main hall. The table was set with four cloths. The first was a thick felted undercloth, or silence cloth. On top of this were two cloths that fell to the ground, and another narrow cloth was laid along the edge of the table on the diners' side to catch food spills and the dirt from greasy wrists. Food was served all at one time off wooden platters; mouths were wiped with bread. By the sixteenth century, the presentation of food had become a more dramatic production. Much like a play in three acts, meals were served in courses. Three tablecloths were laid atop each other, one removed after each course. By the late seventeenth century, tablecloths had become a symbol of cleanliness and purity and were folded into elaborate creases, like windowpanes, but the practice lasted only until the eighteenth century, when linen presses came into fashion.

When the art of furniture-making for the middle classes became more refined in the nineteenth century, hostesses were more inclined to show off the well-polished veneer of the table. Tablecloths began to shrink until they were eventually small flannel squares put underneath plates to protect the table's finish from scratches. The best of the cloths were made in London by a merchant named D'Oyley, hence the Anglicized "doily."

Linens Tips:

• Use 100% cotton napkins at a casual breakfast or lunch. Use linen or damask for a more formal dinner or any meals with guests. Synthetic napkins (and tablecloths) should be avoided because they are less absorbent.

• Dinner napkins range in size from twenty-six-inch squares (very rare) to twenty-two-inch squares. I prefer twenty-four-inch squares for dinner and twenty-two-inch for luncheon. Standard luncheon napkins of twenty inches are too small. If you can afford only one set of napkins, purchase white twenty-four-inch square linen napkins, edged in pullwork or hemstitch, in the heaviest weight possible.

• Napkins and tablecloths do not have to match, but placemats and napkins should.

• Breakfast or lunch tablecloths should hang six to eight inches past the rim of the table. Dinner tablecloths should hang eight to twelve inches over the edge.

Linens Care:

• Never iron stained linens. The hot iron will "cook" the stain into the fabric. Remove any stains before ironing.

• Always dampen linen fabrics before ironing; the fibers are brittle when dry and can be harmed with a hot iron.

• To remove lipstick stains, rub spot with lemon juice. After an hour, place soiled linens in a bath of warm water and bleach (follow label instructions) for five minutes.

• Stains containing proteins (gravy, blood, egg, or ice cream) should be soaked in cold water and bleach.

• To remove candle wax from a tablecloth, harden the wax with ice and remove it with a dull knife.

How to Iron Napkins:

1. After washing linens, dip them in a bath of water and liquid starch, following instructions on the starch label.

2. Wring napkins dry, roll them up, and place in a plastic bag.

3. Refrigerate for at least twenty-four hours.

4. Press with a hot iron. Iron embroidery on the reverse side. Iron damask on the reverse side of pattern nap.

5. Never iron the fold creases in linen; this will stress the fibers. After ironing napkins flat, fold by hand.

KNIVES, FORKS, AND SPOONS

All societies at one time have been in possession of a spoon. Made from bone, stone, wood, gourds, or shells, the spoon is the most basic of forms, modeled on the simple cupped hand. As babies, it is the first flatware we tackle. Pointed sticks for cooking meat were abundant in primitive times, and even crude flint knives were made to cut meat, but for most of our history, food was eaten off the bone or with hands. It wasn't until quite late in the dining scene that the hostess would provide tools to carry food from plate to mouth. Until the mid-eighteenth century, guests would travel with their own spoons and knives (forks were used only to spear food from the serving plate or for cooking), wiping their spoon on a cloth before dipping it into a shared serving bowl. Knives were large, broad, and blunt and used more like a spoon to bring food to the mouth than for cutting. Across the sea in America, it was still acceptable to eat off the blade of a knife until well into the 1850s.

A two-prong hybrid spoon/fork was known in Roman times, but the modern fork didn't make a big splash until the sixteenth century in Spain and Italy. From there it traveled to England, where the fastidious elite admired the tool for keeping dirty fingers out of the mouth. The knife—more associated with weaponry—was eventually dismissed as a tool for peasants or as a symbol of hostility and was to be put by the side of the plate when not in use. From this fashion evolved the elaborate switching back and forth of knife and fork from the ablest hand (the right) that has persisted in America, but not in Europe. It may seem that the noisy switching of knife and fork is the less proper way to handle utensils, but not all agree. To quote Miss Manners: "American table manners are, if anything, a more advanced form of civilized behavior than the European, because they are more complicated and further removed from the practical result, always a sign of refinement."

PLATES

It is strange to think of it now, but the idea of individual place settings is a relative newcomer to table fashion. For centuries, sharing our meat meant also sharing plates and bowls. Once we settled down with woven tablecloths and pronged forks, we decided to define our guests' place at the table by anchoring them with an individual plate. The earliest "plates" were slices of stale bread called "trenchers" (from the French *trancher*, to slice), used to hold food. Often hollowed-out slabs of wood were placed under the trenchers to hold juices. By the sixteenth century, the rectangular trays had morphed into circles made of pewter or other metals. But it wasn't until the seventeenth century in France that flat ceramic plates were seen, and they weren't common tableware until the nineteenth century.

China Care:
• Bone china can scratch; avoid harsh detergents and scouring pads. Rinse as soon after use as possible and wash by hand. Over time, dishwashers will dull the surface of fine china and will damage gold rims or hand painting.
• Do not soak bone china. Water will seep into cracks and cause staining and weakening.
• When storing dishes, stack no more than eight (if possible), with a protective cloth or paper towel between dishes.

GLASS AND CRYSTAL

Blown-glass vessels made an appearance in the Roman Empire in the first century, but most glass production for the next 1,500 years was devoted to making windows. It wasn't until 1660 that an English firm discovered that by adding lead to molten glass a clearer, more crystalline effect could be achieved. Adding lead to the raw materials also yielded a softer glass that could be etched, cut, and ground, allowing the glassmaker to produce more intricate designs able to refract light. From England, the art of making crystal glassware spread to glassmaking centers in Ireland, Czechoslovakia, Bavaria, and France.

Glass and Crystal Care:
• Lead crystal is soft and should never be cleaned with abrasives or put in the dishwasher. Wash by hand with a mild detergent. (Line the sink with a towel to avoid breakage.)
• To remove water stains, soak crystal in a bath of warm water and denture powder.
• Sand small chips on the rim of crystal with an emery board.

THE CENTERPIECE

In eighteenth-century France, the fashion of a table *centre-pièce*, or focal point, hit an extravagant peak. Middleboards, or tiered wooden pyramids called *surtouts*, were placed in the center of the table and crowded with fruits. In England, humbler *surtouts* or *épergnes* of glass, silver, and gold held condiments, fruits, or candles. French nobles at the time would also decorate their tables with intricate sand gardens made of colored sugars and tinted marble dust around which would be placed miniature urns, statues, and fountains made from dough. These perishable wonders were eventually copied in porcelain and silver. Fresh flowers, however, were not considered chic; they were too close to nature and therefore crude and rustic. But fanciful imitations of silk, feathers, or cut vegetables became the rage; it wasn't until the end of the nineteenth century that fresh cut flowers became the centerpiece of choice.

TABLE ACCESSORIES

Over the years I have collected objects to dress the table, such as small boxes, decorated covered dishes, and Staffordshire figurines, and I have found that the table is a perfect place to show them off. (I have never been one to hoard a collection behind glass doors.) It isn't essential that your collection be of antique value, only that the display match the tenor of your table. For instance, a collection of silver snuffboxes would show well on a formal table accessorized with silver flatware, while a collection of miniature books would look well on a table set for a quiet dinner for two.

The most elusive accessory for me has always been good-looking salt and pepper shakers. I keep my eye out for small bowls (crystal, china, bone, silver, or shell) that can serve as cellars, or whimsical figures, such as the artichoke salt and pepper shakers (page 314), that will bring a smile to my guests.

I HAVE CONFINED MY PLATE COLLECTING TO FOUR GROUPS: OCHER, GREEN, BROWN, AND

TAN EARTHENWARE; CREAM COLORS AND OFF-WHITES; TRANSFERWARE FLORALS, AND BLUE AND
WHITE EXPORT OR REPRODUCTION PORCELAIN.

I USE TWO BASIC SETS OF STEMWARE: CLEAR AND ETCHED CRYSTAL, AND A MIX OF COLORED
(MOSTLY COBALT AND CRANBERRY) GLASS.

THE TABLETOP IS A PERFECT PLATFORM TO SHOWCASE MY COLLECTION OF BLUE-AND-WHITE AND STAFFORDSHIRE

CHINA. THROUGH THE YEARS I HAVE KEPT AN EYE OUT FOR WHIMSICAL SALT AND PEPPER SHAKERS, GRINDERS,

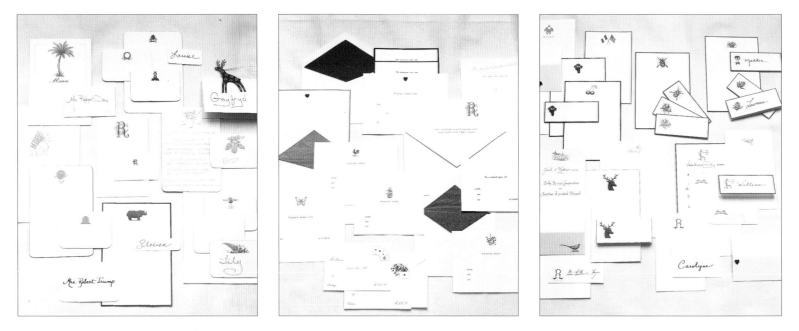

AND CELLARS. INVITATIONS, PLACE CARDS, AND MENU CARDS SHOULD BE MADE OF HEAVY STOCK.

Most of us do not have a huge collection of silver candlesticks, but I would recommend one good pair of plain silver candlesticks tall enough not to be at the eye level of your guests. If you can't afford these, a pair of glass hurricane shades is a stunning addition to either a formal or informal table.

I also make a point of scouring paper and stationery shops for invitations, place cards, and menu cards: The last two I use for formal dinners of more than ten. If it is a large party for friends, I write only first names on the place cards, which I put on the napkin or service plate. I rarely use menu cards unless the meal is exotic, and this card is displayed in front of the host's or hostess's place setting.

Table-setting fashions may have changed over the centuries, and a study of that evolution may explain how we got to the rules we have today, but without a guide (or a knowing grandmother), how are we to learn what goes where? After so many years of going through the motions, I have pared down the table-setting steps to the following:

Table-Setting Walkthrough:

1. To be sure that your table is big enough for the number of guests you are having, measure 24 inches from the center of one place setting to the center of another.

2. Cover the table or tables with a soft felt undercloth or table pad. Place the tablecloth (touch up with an iron before laying the tablecloth if necessary).

3. Place the centerpiece. The centerpiece should be low enough for guests to see across, or tall and thin enough to look through.

4. Space chairs around the table.

5. Lay the service plate, or if it is a less-formal occasion, the dinner plate one inch from the lip of the table. Center the plate with the chair.

6. Put knives and spoons on the right (spoons to the right of knives), and forks to the left of the plate, pointing the edges of the knives toward the plate. (The oyster or seafood fork is the only fork to go on the right, next to the outermost spoon.) Be sure to lay the flatware, turned upward, in the order of use (following the courses of food), beginning from the outside working in. Do not put flatware on the table that will not be used during the meal, no matter how decorative you think it is.

7. Place napkins to the left of the forks or on the center of the service plate. The napkin fold can go to the right or left, but be consistent all around the table.

8. Wineglasses—red and white—and water goblets should be placed at the upper right of the dinner plate, at the tip of the knife, either in ascending order of size or in a triangle of three. Do not put more than three glasses at a place setting.

9. Butter plates—which are appropriate for formal luncheons or casual dinners—are placed above the forks with the butter knife on the plate, parallel to the table.

10. Dessert fork and spoon are placed above the plate. (The coffee spoon should come with the coffee cup on the saucer.)

11. Place salt and pepper shakers or cellars evenly around the table, one set for two guests to share if possible. Place remaining decorative elements. Place candlesticks (to be used only for occasions after dark); they should be tall enough not to shine in the eyes of the diners.

12. With a soft cloth, give the silverware, china, and crystal a final polish.

13. Decide the final seating arrangements, write the place cards, and put a place card on top of the napkin (if on the service plate) or on or above the service plate itself.

Table-Setting Pet Peeves:

• Fussy and distracting napkin rings
• Elaborate napkin folding
• Scented candles on the table that interfere with the aroma of the food
• Polyester or synthetic linens
• Clunky stems on wine glasses at formal dinners
• Dark napkins
• Overcrowded tabletops
• Jars, bottles, or cartons on the table. (Decant all condiments and drinks. No labels on the table!)
• Badly pressed linens and puckering at hemstitch lines
• Printed tablecloths at formal dinners
• Fussy, overdone centerpieces and too many decorations cluttering the table
• Overexaggerated tabletop themes (never let the complexity of the tabletop surpass the quality of the food)
• Absence of place cards, unless the dinner is for fewer than ten

The Key Elements of Design

COLOR

When we're faced with any design challenge, color—more than texture or proportion—provokes the greatest insecurity. Most of us seem unsure what shades mix well together. In the preceding pages I have shown you some of my favorite color pairings (blue and white, celadon and pink, white and red), but it is the subtleties of shade that intimidate. To understand and appreciate color takes time and study. The best way to learn how to use color is simple: look. Elementary as this may sound, most of us do not really focus on the color around us. We take it for granted, and absorb its presence on an unconscious level. We need to sharpen our vision when exploring imaginative ways to use color. Two excellent guides are great artists and nature. Eighteenth-century rococo painters such as Fragonard and Boucher, or the bolder work of modernists such as Matisse, Kandinsky, and Hockney, provide excellent examples of keen color sense. I have kept numerous files over the years filled with museum postcards and pictures cut from magazines; whenever I see an image that enchants me, it goes into the file. When I need inspiration, I refer to the file. I have also become an enthusiastic, if not particularly accomplished, photographer of gardens and flowers. These images remind me of the colors that nature provides. Trust her. She is rarely wrong.

If you are not one of the rare breed who know instinctively what colors combine pleasingly, it is also helpful to learn the basics of color theory. Begin with a color wheel, available at any art-supply house. (Also helpful: a plump book of color chips available from paint manufacturers.) Hundreds of books have been written about the science of the spectrum that are more exhaustive on the topic, but in short: Each primary color (red, blue, and yellow) has a secondary color (green, orange, and purple) that lies directly opposite on a color wheel. The secondary color is the complement of the primary color. For instance, green is the complement of red, orange is the complement of blue, and purple is the complement of yellow. Since complementary colors enhance the value of primary colors, they make vibrant bedfellows, as do their tints (the colors plus white) and shades (the color plus black). Analogous colors, which are any three touching colors on a wheel, also make lively combinations: red, yellow, and orange; blue, purple, and green; blue-violet, turquoise, and chartreuse. Monochromatic color schemes (this is where the paint chips come in handy), those created with one color and its tints and shades, evoke a more sedate setting. Whether you choose to employ an analogous, monochromatic, or complementary color scheme, it is important to remember that color dictates the mood of your table. If you consciously study color and its effects on your table designs, eventually your own personal style emerges.

TEXTURE

Once your color scheme is decided, the next consideration is more elusive, but just as important. Texture gives underlying structure to the table. Setting a table without considering the textures of

EASTER IN THE COUNTRY   PAGE 25   A PARISIAN DINNER   PAGE 32   AN EARLY LUNCH   PAGE 45

MOTHER'S DAY   PAGE 48   A BIRTHDAY CELEBRATION   PAGE 219   A THANKSGIVING START   PAGE 224

A BIRTHDAY DINNER   PAGE 281   AN IMPROMPTU LUNCH   PAGE 288   A VALENTINE'S DAY DINNER   PAGE 295

the tablecloth, glasses, plates, flowers, and stemware deprives the scene of an ineffable weightiness. Textures can be shiny, dull, woven, velvety, rough, sheer, and on and on. Also like color, texture can be matched with like texture (lattice-etched crystal and diamond-quilted matelassé cloth) or paired with its opposing complement (the ripped saw-toothed edges of carnations juxtaposed with minimal sleek white china). The detailing of china and textile patterns should not clash; it is better that they borrow from each other. The ivy rim of plates matching an ivy centerpiece is an obvious example. The scalloped edge of a linen napkin next to a similar scalloped rim of a plate is another. Attention to the marriage of textures of table, linens, china, and flowers will help you create a more interesting table.

Texture also speaks to mood. As a rule, rough unfinished surfaces suit rustic scenes; highly polished surfaces fit formal settings. But mixing the two also has charming effects. Carved and upholstered dining room chairs add grace to a beaten-up farm table, just as worn café chairs erase the solemnity of a highly polished walnut table.

The detailing of china and textile patterns should not clash; it is better that they borrow from each other.

PROPORTION

If you look closely at some of the tables in this book, you will see a pattern of proportion. The center of the table will have the largest focal point (the bouquet or centerpiece), which often will be surrounded by smaller replicas—or some repeated elements—of the same arrangement, followed by even smaller elements (the plates and flatware). Other tables may adhere to a more linear configuration, with the floral focal point being a level line of flowers or plants occupying the center of the table. Both tables, the triangular arrangement and the linear arrangement, obey the same proportion of scale: Largest thing stands in center while accessories diminish in size to the edge of the table. Much of this configuration is due to practicality; big things in the middle are apt to be out of the way of elbows, but it also has to do with harmony. It seems right to the eye. If you study the layouts of art-directed tables in home-decorating magazines, other equations of proportion will be revealed. It is simply a matter of observation and digestion: You must know what you are looking for before you can detect a deliberate pattern. Some may argue, but there is no hard-and-fast rule of scale—I tend to err on the side of bigger centerpiece is better—and you need only be aware that such a thing exists and affects the cohesion and mood you are trying to achieve. Most important when considering proportion, remember not to think of your table as an island in a vacuum. The surrounding space, the environment, should be considered. The height of the ceiling demands that you adjust the scale of the tabletop, just as the backdrop—where the table is situated—affects the style of the table décor. Consider the entire environment in which your play will be staged before inviting the players to come to the table.

Recipe Index

A

Apple Cake with Apple Cider Glaze, 234
Apple Pear Crisp, 237
Asparagus with Lemon Confit, 87
Asparagus in Puff Pastry with Lemon Sauce, 78
Asparagus, Veal, and Prosciutto Bundles, 154
Aunt June's Lemon Bars, 83

B

Baker's® Chocolate Pecan Pie Bars, 162
Barbecued Baby Back Ribs, 161
Basic Tart Dough, 159
Berries and Red Currants with Grand Marnier Sauce, 82
Biscuit Sandwiches of Mustard-Glazed Ham and Smoked Cheddar, 82
Blueberry Rhubarb Pie, 159
Brussels Sprouts with Pancetta and Cream, 242

C

California Fried Onion Rings, 157
Caramelized Bananas with Toasted Coconut and Lime, 81
Carolyne's Favorite Sugar Cookies, 302
Carrot Leek Soup with Orange Essence, 155
Coconut Cake, 89
Corn Soup with Red Pepper Purée, 303
Cumin-Scented Asparagus Soup, 86

D

Daire's Fudgy Rum Chocolate Cake, 157
Dandelion Greens with Bacon and Garlic, 85
David's Squash Soup, 240

F

Fresh Mozzarella, Tomato, and Pesto Salad, 162

G

Game Bird Pot Pie, 234
Game Hens with Dried Plum Stuffing, 236
Grandma Beaty's Homemade Noodles, 242
Green Cauliflower Soup with Pita Triangles, 79
Grilled Spicy Moroccan Chicken with Quinoa, 87
Grilled Swordfish with Artichokes, Tomatoes, and Olives, 304

J

Jalapeño Corn Muffins, 238
Jeanne's Asian Coleslaw, 161

L

Lemon-Dill Pasta Salad with Shrimp and Grapes, 156

M

Margarida's Frittata, 84
Margarida's Portuguese Clams, 86

N

Nancy's Black Bean Chili, 238

O

Orange Pecan Waffles, 240
Otha's Pound Cake, 302

P

Pear Ginger Pie, 239
Pear Mango Salsa, 85
Pecan Tarts, 235
Pork Loin with Kumquats, 303
Potatoes Anna, 81

R

Red Velvet Cake, 155
Rigatoni with Summer Vegetables, 158
Roasted Capon with Corn Bread Stuffing, 241
Roasted Leg of Lamb Marinated with Fresh Herbs, 80

S

Seafood en Papillote, 163
Seared Sesame Tuna with Pear-Mango Salsa, 84
Short Ribs with Spicy Lemon Caper Sauce, 236
Shrimp and White Bean Soup, 305
Smoky Cumin Chicken, 159
Strawberry Pavlova, 79
Strawberry Rhubarb Sorbet, 154
Susan's Cranberry Relish, 243
Sweet Potato and Pear Soup, 305

T

Three-Berry Pie, 160

V

Veal Scallops with Morels and Cream, 78

W

Weatherstone Fried Chicken, 160
White Bean and Shrimp Salad, 88

Z

Zucchini and Watercress Soup, 88

No project can be fully realized without the special help of many. Grateful thanks to Sylvie, not only a colleague, but also a dear friend as well, who did the lion's share of the beautiful photography in this book. Thanks also to the three other gifted photographers: Alan Richardson, Anne Day, and Eric Bowman. An enormous thank you to all of the Weatherstone staff: Placido, Susan, and Margarida, who ironed, cleaned, lugged tables, cut flowers, helped arrange flowers, and decorated with me for all of the holidays.

To Nancy, the head cook at Weatherstone, whose great culinary talents, along with Margarida's, have added ten pounds I don't regret to my waist and hips. Also thanks to Aunt June, Mom, and Grandma Beaty for family recipes. Thank you to my good friend David Monn for his friendship, his delicious squash soup, and his red velvet cake recipe.

ACKNOWLEDGMENTS

As a visual person, a designer, written words are difficult for me, so thanks and congratulations to Melissa Davis for deciphering my scribbling and putting my thoughts into intelligent and elegant prose. Thanks to Molly McCarthy in New York for helping us out in every way.

Thanks to the gardeners Joanne and Marcus, who provided flowers, fruits, and vegetables for the Weatherstone tables.

To Dina, whose elegant good taste is evident throughout every page.

To Cullen Stanley, my agent, who has found a great new home for my books. To Jennifer Josephy, my editor at Broadway Books, who worked so hard to get this book ready in a very short time.